Gospel Culture

The Cultural Markings of a Christ-Centered Church

HOPE EAST QUEENS PUBLISHING

David S. Jung

HOPE EAST QUEENS PUBLISHING

Gospel Culture
Copyright © 2018 by David S. Jung

This title is also available as an eBook

Requests for information should be addressed to:
Hope East Queens, 39-24 Bell Boulevard, Bayside, New York 11361
E-mail: eastqueens@hopechurchnyc.org

Hope East Queens Publishing® is the book-publishing division of Hope East Queens®, a Christ-centered Christian community in Bayside, New York. All proceeds from this title go to Hope East Queens. For more information, write to 39-24 Bell Boulevard, Bayside, New York 11361, or visit the website at https://www.hopeeastqueens.org.

Original and modified cover art by NaCDS and CoverDesignStudio.com.

ISBN-13: 978-1537287119
ISBN-10: 1537287117

First Print April 2018 / Printed in the United States of America

Acknowledgements

I am forever indebted to God our father for showing me the love that inspired me to write. Without His love, my words are only a resounding gong and a clanging cymbal (1 Corinthians 13:1).

I would like to acknowledge Jany, my amazing wife and best friend; thank you for your kindness, love, and patience. Emmett and Lucy, my two beautiful children, you help me every day to become a better man. To my mother, who gave everything for my family, you are the most sacrificial human being I know.

Thank you to the *Hope East Queens* family. Because God brought such remarkable people into my life, I will never forget that His plans are bigger than my own. Thank you, Andrew Hyun, for believing in me and being crazy enough to take a chance. Thank you, Brad Williams and Peter Bonanno, for all your support as partners in Christ. Thanks to Maria W. Kim, for your remarkable insight. Thanks to my editor, Noelia Chung; you are truly a gift from God. And to everyone else who inspired me to just keep going, sincerely I say, *thank you.*

Contents

Introduction

True story: Soon after I signed the lease to the location of our prospective church plant in Bayside, Queens (just six months prior to our first Sunday service), I discovered another pastor had subsequently visited that very same location and offered the owner *more* money to start his own church there, fully knowing we already had a lease in place. Thankfully, the owner chose to honor our agreement, but for a while I felt deeply resentful that someone who professed to be a man of faith would do such a thing. It was then I came to the alarming realization that I too could one day walk down that same self-seeking path. The Lord challenged me to search my heart and reflect on my own ambitions. Why was I really planting this church? Was it to build God's kingdom or my own?

Which brings us to April 17, 2016, only our second Sunday preview service for Hope East Queens. I felt convicted to deliver a message that was a bit of a risk for someone who was supposed to be painting a memorable first impression. I knew it was a risk because I had given portions of this message during my final presentation for my one-year church planting training and received mostly negative feedback for it being too "uninspiring". (To be fair, I may have thought the same if I were a church planting expert/strategist.) But that's how I knew the conviction was from the Lord, because it made no sense to go through with it otherwise. I started the message (to be accurate, it was more like a vision statement) rather predictably, quoting the Great

Commission (Matthew 28:18-20) and talking about how we as Christians are called to reach the unreached. Thus, church plants are essential because they are effective vehicles for sharing the gospel with non-believers.

After about fifteen minutes of explaining the need for new churches, the natural next step was to make some grandiose claim about how I believed God had "great" things in store for Hope East Queens and how this was a golden opportunity for everyone to hop on board the ride. (I tend to place into quotations anything I feel could be in danger of our subjective, rather than Biblical, definitions.) After all, based on my prior church experiences, the best way for church leaders to inspire people to come, give, and get involved was to talk about the "great" things God had planned for the church, sometimes stated as "God's moving". Now, I'm sure many of those messages were delivered with sincerity and good intentions, and I'm in no way implying that people should not get involved with their church. I am only pointing out that doing God's work should not primarily be motivated by a desire to see evidence of God's moving. Rather, what should motivate us is what He has *already* done through the cross, and we gather as the Lord's people to celebrate this good news with our worship to God and service to others.

Thus, in my opinion, it is a cheap trick for a pastor to stand in the front at one's second Sunday gathering and bait people into joining his/her church with promises of "great" things. The truly great things have already taken place, we merely gather as the Lord's people to celebrate such good news with our worship to God and service towards others.

And so, with the Lord's conviction, I nervously switched gears, and during only our second Sunday service ever, instead of selling people on how great Hope East Queens was going to be, I went against the counsel of those wiser and more experienced than me and began to describe the ways in which we would not, and could not, compete with other churches.

We couldn't be the best church in New York City if we tried; Timothy Keller of Redeemer Presbyterian Church already ensured that I would not be the best speaker, and Carl Lentz of Hillsong NYC certainly ensured that I would not be the best-looking pastor.

All kidding aside, people like being the "best," including being at the "best" church. But what does it mean to be the "best" church anyway? Is it the church with the highest attendance? Does it mean to have the nicest facility? Smoothest Sunday presentation? The most attractive website or active social media accounts? Excellence in preaching? In worship? In welcoming practices? In programs and systems? In children's ministries?

What if to be the "best" church in the eyes of man means that pastors, leaders, staff members, and volunteers must drain themselves of their emotional, physical, and spiritual health because of their obsession with being the "best?" What if to be the "best" means to forego love and intimacy with God, our primary calling in life?

"Teacher, which is the greatest commandment in the Law?" Jesus replied: 'Love the Lord your God with all your heart and with all your soul and with all your mind.'" (Matthew 22:36-37)

Kristian Hernandez, the man who succeeded Andrew ("Drew") Hyun as the lead pastor of Hope Church Astoria (the first branch of our network of churches), once preached rather boldly at a planters gathering, "Ministry fruit is not evidence of the fruit of the Spirit," and that "it is possible to do the work of God without intimacy with God."[1] I mentioned that he preached rather boldly because it is not easy to tell a hundred and fifty driven church planters that their ambitions, goals, and dreams, if not properly evaluated, may actually be coming from a place of darkness.

Too often, we let the world's standards dictate what a "great" church should look like. I once heard Peter Ahn, lead pastor of Metro Community Church in Englewood Cliffs, New Jersey, share about how he had started an initiative where the church would bus in kids from the inner city for the youth group's Friday night service.[2] Unfortunately, there was a tremendous backlash from the church members. Many parents did not want to send their privileged teens to the same youth group as the underprivileged kids. Some church members even gave Peter an ultimatum; the church could either stop the initiative or they would find a new church to attend.

7

Eventually, Peter addressed the issue from the pulpit and informed his congregation that if they refused to send their kids to the youth group because of the inner-city outreach, they should leave and find another church because loving the poor and the oppressed was a part of their church DNA and that would not change. He said, "I'm sorry, but we can't stop reaching out to them; those kids are our family too." As a result, many church members left, including some big tithers and some who had been a part of Metro Community Church since its founding. The church took a significant hit financially and in its membership, but Peter continued to stick with his convictions.

If doing church is a business, Peter made a monumental blunder. He could easily have kept on pleasing people and few would have questioned his leadership. His membership and tithing would have continued to increase, and the kingdom of Metro Community Church would have grown. But doing church is not a business. The church is the body of Christ, and the success of a church is not measured by the world's standards.

It's time we put our worldly views of being the "best" aside and do God's work the way in which *He* intended. After all, the first century church did not grow because of the bright lights of church excellence or by trying to measure up to the world's standards of excellence. Instead, it was the radical transformation through the gospel message that moved people's hearts to organically spread the good news wherever they went.

"Day after day, in the temple courts and from house to house, they never stopped teaching and proclaiming the good news that Jesus is the Messiah." (Acts 5:42)

Furthermore, not only was Hope East Queens not going to be the best church in New York City (by the world's standard), we weren't going to try to compete with other churches at all. Dietrich Bonhoeffer in *Life Together* puts it best:

"Life together under the Word will remain sound and healthy only where it does not form itself into a movement, an order, a society, but rather where it understands itself as

being a part of the one, holy, Christian church, where it shares actively and passively in the sufferings and struggles and promise of the *whole* Church."[3]

The above statement blew my mind when I first read it. In 1939, Bonhoeffer was addressing the same issues of individual church pride and competition that continue to infect churches to this day. Perhaps if Christians took Bonhoeffer's words to heart we'd have healthier churches today. Imagine that as a truth, we should never view our own church or movement as existing outside of the one whole Christian church. We are all *one* with Christ as our head; there are no churches of Hillsong NYC or Redeemer Presbyterian Church, and there are no churches of Hope Church NYC or denominational networks. There is only the **"one, holy, Christian church."[4]** We are not simply called to love our own church that we attend on Sunday, we are called to love *the* church.

As previously mentioned, I grew up in churches that inspired members to do the Lord's work by telling them that their churches were somehow better than the others, often manipulating and exaggerating truths in the hope of creating a movement. It blew my mind that pastors and leaders could be so blind to the arrogance and the spirit of divisiveness that this leadership method was cultivating in their congregations. Over time, I grew cynical and I began to doubt whether humans could ever do church successfully without being motivated by their own selfish pride and ambition.

Then I met Drew Hyun, the founder of the Hope Church NYC network, who sat a group of ambitious church planters down one Monday morning and stated quite frankly, "I say this in the presence of God, we are not here to build an empire or our own brand, we are here solely for His kingdom." Ironically, he was saying this during a time when there was significant forward momentum in our respective churches.

Then I met Timothy Keller, founding pastor of Redeemer Presbyterian Church in Manhattan, who recently spoke to me about how he planned to dedicate the remainder of his life to raising money to help church plants of different denominations in cities all over the world. Furthermore, Redeemer continues to train and partner with new planters every year through their Redeemer City to City organization rather than funneling money and resources into expanding their own brand.[5]

Then I met Finney Varughese, lead pastor of Hope Church Long Island in Hempstead, New York, who when Drew had the Hope Church pastors lay hands on me to pray for our new church plant, earnestly spoke out loud, "Dear God, please let Hope East Queens have *more* people than Hope Long Island."

Then I received numerous anonymous donations from outsiders for our church with simple messages such as, "Hallelujah! We love what you are doing, brother!"

At first, I had difficulty comprehending why pastors would downplay or detract attention away from their own movements, brands, and/or achievements in favor of others, or pray for others to succeed in ministry even more than themselves, or why people would anonymously give to churches they weren't even affiliated with (church or denomination-wise). The only conclusion I came up with is this: they weren't living for their own kingdoms, they were living for someone else's, His Kingdom. Like Bonhoeffer, they wanted to share in the struggles and promises of the whole Church.

To my surprise, it was this seemingly counterintuitive message I gave that April Sunday in 2016, and not some inspirational message about how amazing Hope East Queens was going to be, that brought out the most positive response I had ever received for a sermon. Like me, many people were tired of being told to join a church because then they would be part of something "great". Instead, they wanted to hear the good news that we are already worthy and redeemed because of Christ's atoning sacrifice on the cross. I realized that perhaps my cynicism wasn't entirely warranted, and that there were still many Christians who still deeply longed for a church whose values and culture were centered on God's greatness, and not our own.

Through the process of prayerfully planting a church with gospel-centeredness in mind, I came up with seven values I believe are essential to a church that wants to cultivate a gospel culture that's focused on building God's Kingdom rather than our own. Perhaps there are others, but these are the seven I wish to discuss here in depth.

Christ at the Center

Putting Christ at the center of the church is at the core of all the values we're going to discuss, and yet, it is also the most difficult to model really well. In this chapter I will discuss three important markers of a truly Christ-centered church. First, a Christ-centered church is not dependent on any single person. Secondly, in a Christ-centered church, we relate to the gospel. Lastly, in a Christ-centered church, people are motivated to love and serve others by the gospel, instead of being motivated by fear, shame and/or pride.

1. A Christ-centered church is not dependent on any single person.

If I were to ask someone to say the first thing that comes to mind about a well-known church, most people would probably say the name of the lead pastor. And yet, according to Scripture, *Jesus Christ* is supposed to be the focal point of the church.

"And God placed all things under [Jesus'] feet and appointed him to be head over everything for the church, which is *his body*, the fullness of him who fills everything in every way." (Ephesians 1:22-23)

11

Most of us have grown so accustomed to this pastor-centric church culture that it's difficult to even begin to conceptualize what a truly Christ-centered church would look like. This tendency to place a person at the center of a church's identity doesn't just apply to congregation members. Church leaders are just as guilty, often to the detriment of the congregations they are tasked to lead.

My personal story of blindness and ignorance as a Christian leader comes from my five years as a youth pastor. During that time, I had to coordinate two services and give two separate messages every week (Fridays and Sundays). For the first three years, after every Friday evening service, I drove the church van to drop kids off all over Queens, and sometimes Long Island. Afterwards, I'd have to bring the van back to the church (in Queens) and drive my own car home (to Long Island). On my worst days, I would return to my house past two o'clock in the morning. I eventually grew so bitter that some nights I took the church van home with me, only to get a call at five o'clock in the morning asking me to bring it back because it was needed for Saturday morning prayer service pickups. Such were the expectations of the youth pastor by the church at the time, but I was too stubborn, prideful, and timid to try to change the culture by asking others for help.

On Sundays, I led teacher meetings before service, prepared and substituted in for Bible study classes whenever teachers were absent, then ran over to participate in meetings with parents or the education department, and still found time to fellowship with the kids afterwards with sports, meals, and games. Heck, I even came extra early on Sundays to attend worship team practices (just to spectate, as I knew absolutely nothing about music).

During those five years, I missed Sunday service a grand total of two times. The first time I was absent for my honeymoon, and the second, I had to attend a continuing legal education course to uphold my law degree (but even then, I drove to church afterwards just for the sake of showing my face–sadly, there was no one left to see it).

However, none of that compared to how obsessive I was about attending every church event possible, and not just the major events such as church picnics, retreats, and worship nights. When there were grade outings, I was there. When teachers would grab dinner, I was there. I spoke at students' school Christian clubs and frequently took kids out for meals. And yes, a part of me did these things because I loved the kids (I really did), but another part me just didn't trust anyone else to do them. Rather than delegating some of these tasks to others, I considered myself indispensable to the health and success of the ministry.

If I'm being honest, I also wanted people to acknowledge that I was doing a "good" job. And for most of those five years, there was no doubt in my mind that I was, in fact, doing a "good" job. Why? Because everyone around me appeared to think so. I heard endlessly about how all the students and parents raved about me. My mother would even hear such news whenever our church members would visit her store. If I'm to be honest, it all felt pretty darn good; it was an addictive feeling and it only motivated me to go harder.

However, six months before I stepped down because of burnout, my body was overwhelmed with feelings of anxiety and I had trouble sleeping at night. When I prayed and self-reflected, I realized it was due to the fear/horror of knowing how ill-prepared the church was to handle my departure. Suddenly, I was filled with regret.

Although I was doing a good job in the eyes of man, I actually did a bad job in the eyes of God. Instead of pointing others to Christ, which is what I was called to do as a pastor, I had been elevating myself in the eyes of man. In my pride, arrogance, and desire to feel valued and wanted, I placed myself at the center of the ministry instead of Christ. Perhaps, by refraining from showing up to every event imaginable and allowing other leaders and members to step up in my stead, my own legacy would have been diminished. But it would have been diminished for the greater good, to highlight the legacy of the one whose sandal straps I am not worthy to even untie (John 1:27).

You see, I am still not an expert in conceptualizing and realizing a Christ-centered church, far from it. But I now know this for a fact: if a pastor leaves and the church cannot function as well or even nearly as well, then Christ is not at the center of that ministry.

Putting Christ at the center must be a shared vision of *both* leaders and congregation members. Pastors and leaders should not set themselves apart as being indispensable to a ministry, and church members should not have such expectations. Scripture describes the body of Christ as having various parts and functions, but each part should have equal concern for each other (1 Corinthians 12:22-25).

I was able to see this principle in action while I was still serving my one-year pastoral residency (prior to planting) under Kristian Hernandez at Hope Church Astoria. One day, a desperate lady once approached me after service and asked for the lead pastor's prayers because there was a chance she could have breast cancer. I quickly ran down the stairs and found Kristian, who was busy conducting a meeting. When he asked me what I needed, I informed him of the lady's request and then told him that I would tell her to wait until he was finished. As I was walking out the door, he suggested an alternative, "Or, I have a better idea, David. Why don't *you* pray for her?"

And so I did. Till this day I'm thankful Kristian allowed me to because if the lead pastor, or any other pastor for that matter, is the only person in the church who can pray for someone who is ill or potentially ill, then once again, Christ is not at the center of that ministry. In a Christ-centered church, all members of his body possess the ability to pray and intercede for others (1 Timothy 2:1).

Furthermore, in some churches, the pastor simply tells everyone what to do or not to do with their lives, but that should not be the goal of a leader in a Christ-centered church. Although pastoral guidance, wisdom, and accountability is important for a congregation's growth, church leaders should be encouraging their members to cultivate their own relationship with Christ so that through prayer, reading the Word, and self-reflection, they can make decisions on their own that are pleasing to Him. Therefore, it is essential that leaders don't emphasize loyalty to pastors or the church, but rather they stress intimacy with Jesus. This way, people don't make life decisions solely based on a pastor's word or their sense of loyalty to him/her or the church. Instead, they learn how to discern Christ's will themselves through developing and deepening their own personal relationship with him. The only way to accomplish this is by encouraging people to focus on what matters – the *gospel*.

2. In a Christ-centered church we relate to the gospel.

While I was still working as a youth pastor, the education department pastor had all the church pastors and teachers come into a classroom one Sunday afternoon and asked us, "What is the gospel in a nutshell?" Everyone, nearly forty education department leaders, went dead silent all at once, no one wanting to give the wrong answer and risk looking foolish in front of the group.

Now, if I asked those people that same question individually, they would have answers, beautiful answers, answers that came from their heart and were rich with feelings of love, security, and hope. Furthermore, each person's response to the question would likely differ in some form or another, because the truth is there is no single all-encompassing answer to that question. Even when the Bible itself tries to summarize the gospel it comes out looking different each time (John 3:16, 1 Corinthians 15:1-8, 2 Corinthians 5:14-19, Titus 2:11-14). The news of Christ's righteous life, unjust death, and victorious resurrection is always the same, but the way it relates to us individually can vary. Simply put, different people hear and relate to the gospel differently because, well, we're all different. In that way, the gospel is both simple yet extremely complex.

For example, self-loathing people who struggle with self-esteem issues hear in the gospel just how special they are in God's eyes; so special that He would sacrifice His one and only son for them (John 3:16), and so valued that He would leave the ninety-nine in pursuit of them (Matthew 18:12-14).

Those who see God as a distant figure because of His divine nature (or doubt that He's there at all) hear in the gospel that He came to earth as one of us, walked with us, bled, wept, and suffered with us, and in doing so, has demonstrated that He is a God who understands our pains and relates to our struggles (Isaiah 53:3-4).

People who feel as though they are too much of a sinner to be accepted by God hear in the gospel that salvation is free. Jesus Christ already lived the righteous life that we should have lived, and likewise died the death we should have died on the cross. Thus, they can go to Him freely regardless of their sins (Ephesians 3:12).

On the other hand, those who feel Christ's sacrifice now allows them a free pass to live a life of self-indulgence and debauchery hear that the gospel is a message filled with so much grace that no one could possibly accept it and not at the very least repent and desire to live a godly life in return (Mark 1:15, Romans 2:4).

And of course, self-righteous Christians hear in the gospel that they did absolutely nothing to earn salvation for themselves, that Jesus Christ did all the work in their stead, and therefore, they should come down off their high horses and into a world of humility (2 Corinthians 12:9-10).

On my first day of church planting training with Redeemer City to City, the six of us in the group were asked to write down a concise definition of the gospel in our own words. Unfortunately, I had a bit of a brain freeze. When it came to pastoring and preaching, I could always do it with confidence, but when it came to being evaluated in any manner whatsoever by authority figures, I was downright horrendous. And so as time was running out, I stared in a daze at my blank sheet of paper while the others in the group vigorously scribbled away. When time was up, they asked us to read aloud our answers–I went last. The first five all had terrific answers, they used powerful words like incarnational, restoration, sacramental, etc.

When it came to my turn, this is what I showed them:

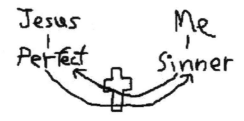

"Uh, do you care to explain this David?" I was asked by the instructor.

"Jesus was perfect, I was a sinner, and at the cross we switched," I replied, and then added, "Oh, and that makes me *really* love him."

Of course, it wasn't the most intellectual or impressive answer, but it was the answer that resonated the most with me. After all, the gospel must be explained in a manner that moves us, not just intellectually, but at our inmost being where it matters most. Simple as it seems, the above illustration moves my heart. It is when the gospel ceases to be simply head knowledge that we can experience the full transforming power of the good news, bringing me to my final point.

3. In a Christ-centered church, we are motivated by the gospel rather than fear, shame, and/or pride.

In the book of Genesis (3:1-13), Adam and Eve disobeyed God by eating the fruit from the tree of the knowledge of good and evil after God specifically instructed them not to. After their disobedience, a few key things entered the world. First, they felt naked for the first time and covered themselves up (v.7). *Shame* entered the world. Second, Adam explained to God, **"I heard you in the garden and I was afraid..."** (v.10). *Fear* entered the world. Lastly, Adam blamed Eve, Eve then blamed the Serpent, and no one was willing to own up to their individual mistakes (v.11-13). *Pride* entered the world. So the Bible gives us a clear understanding from its outset that shame, fear and pride entered the world as a result of sin (disobedience to God).

When I was in high school, I asked my Bible study teacher, "Is being a good Christian because I love Jesus the same as being a good Christian because I am afraid of going to hell?" My teacher answered, "Yes, because they both lead to the same results, being a good Christian."

The *results*. So, are the results what truly matters? Because if that's the case, the Pharisees were putting out some pretty darn good results. After all, they were moral, law-abiding, and gave to the temple treasury. And yet, Jesus was constantly rebuking them, not for their results, but for what was going on inside of their prideful hearts.

"Blind Pharisee! First clean the inside of the cup and dish, and then the outside also will be clean." (Matthew 23:26)

Let's stay with the *results* for a moment. If we're being honest, many of the greatest achievements in human history were usually accomplished through using shame, fear and/or pride as the primary motivators. For example, Charlemagne expanded the Holy Roman Empire using violent methods that forced many in the late eighth and early ninth centuries to convert to Christianity out of shame and fear. The Mongols, the largest dynasty recorded in history, conquered most of Eurasia in the thirteenth century with warriors that were drilled with a strong sense of pride.

The exception to the rule is early Christians who were motivated by the gospel, the good news that brought rich and poor, outwardly and inwardly broken, and Jews and Gentiles together despite harsh persecution. Suddenly, the "sinners" could break bread with the "religious." *Shame* had been broken. When facing religious persecution, instead of being afraid, Christians rejoiced **"...in the hope of the glory of God"** (Romans 5:2). They had been set free from *fear*. Centuries of traditions of ethnocentrism that created divisions between race, socioeconomic class, and gender suddenly didn't matter (Galatians 3:28). *Pride* no longer had the power to cause divisions.

If shame, fear, and pride are all things that entered this world as a result of sin (disobedience to God), then how can they be the way to the gospel? How can they lead us to a reconciliation with God? The answer is they cannot. As we saw in the early Christian church, the gospel was meant to shatter such things that have strongholds in our lives and which keep us far from God.

For practical purposes, if we wanted to commence a church giving campaign to feed hungry children, what would that look like? Well, if the results are all we really care about, here are the quickest ways to get them:

Shame-based motivation would say something like, "We aren't doing enough as Christians! We simply need to do more! We have so much and they have so little. How can we just sit here in our comfortable chairs and do absolutely nothing while these poor children starve? We need to give now!"

Fear-based motivation may go something like this, "When we get to the gates of heaven and see the face of God, aren't you worried about what you'll say when He asks you what you've done for Him? We need to help feed these poor children so that you can confidently tell God that you did His work when you see Him face to face!"

Pride-based motivation may possibly say, "Let's be the church that actually makes a difference in this world, let's lead the way! Let's

18

show others how it's done so that when they see our church they'll be amazed at all the good work we're doing for God's kingdom!"

But *gospel*-based motivation is unlike any of these three. You see, to be motivated by the gospel, one cannot just have some transient moment of shame, fear, or pride, but he/she must be genuinely transformed by a message such as this: "See these poor starving children? What we need to realize is that because of sin, we were once poor and starving spiritually and destined for death as our punishment. But Jesus Christ had tremendous compassion on us, he picked us up out of our own helplessness, and because of his (undeserved) love we are now clothed with royalty. *That* is why we should now have compassion on others. Let's help these poor children because he has first helped us!"

The gospel tells us that our sin problems were even worse than these children's hunger problems, and until we can see ourselves in a more desperate position than them and understand that Jesus Christ compassionately lifts us out with his sacrifice, we cannot experience gospel-motivated compassion.

To illustrate, when I was seventeen years old and hanging out with the wrong crowd, I once conspired with a group of friends to rob a pool hall at one o'clock in the morning. There was only one worker inside at the time, an average-sized Korean-American employee in his mid-twenties manning the cash register. And since I was the only Korean-American in my group, the plan was for me to befriend the man and lead him outside while the others remained inside and broke open the cash register.

After we went in, the others casually shot pool while I began to dialogue with the man just as planned. I told him some of my background story so that we could connect, that my parents got divorced when I was only six and I never had a consistent older male figure to look up to (all true). I could sense that the man felt a deep sense of empathy towards me as he compassionately spoke in Korean with a warm smile saying, "I'll be like your older brother; just come to me if you ever need anything." *Yes! The plan is working!* He was a kind and trusting man, but I was toying with him like a devilish snake.

I told him I needed to have a cigarette and asked if he could follow me out to continue our conversation. We both stepped outside, and as I was carefully lighting my cigarette the man looked inside through the glass and noticed the others attempting to break open the cash register with a crowbar. He then looked at me, we made eye contact momentarily, and in that fleeting second, I recognized in his stunned eyes the horrified look of betrayal.

I reacted in the only way I knew how, I turned around and ran. I ran away as fast I could for several blocks, and then casually began to stroll my way home when I felt I was in the clear. After a few minutes, I recognized a set of bright sirens following me. *Aw man.* Two officers got out of their vehicle and placed me up against the wall to be searched. As you could imagine, I was a teenager scared out of my young mind; I had never been detained by the police before. *This isn't happening. This isn't happening.*

"Hey buddy, ya goin' somewhere at this time of the night?" one of them asked, as he swung me around to face him once they finished their search.

"Just going for a walk sir," I politely responded, while my hundred-and-thirty-pound body was noticeably shaking with trepidation.

"Your parents know you's out this late?"

"Yeah." I then quickly changed my mind to make it sound more plausible. "Well nah, I snuck out."

"You know, you fit perfectly the description of an attempted pool hall robbery we just got word of," the other informed me, as he snickered. I then realized, like a moron, I was wearing a distinct bright neon yellow jacket. "Get inside the car kid." *Darn it.*

They then put me into the backseat and drove me back to the pool hall so that I could be identified. The drive was only a few minutes but it seemed like forever. It was like a bad dream and I kept on pinching myself hoping I'd wake up. When they brought me out of the vehicle, the pool hall cashier was already standing outside with his arms sternly folded. I was so ashamed, I could barely look him in the eyes.

"Is this the guy?" one of the officers asked him.

The man gazed at me for a few seconds with what I initially perceived to be a haughty grin of disgust and so many thoughts rushed through my mind all at once; my life was ruined, and I had brought shame to my family. He then slowly shook his head in disapproval, just like an older brother would when their kid brother does something stupid, snorted out loud, and much to my surprise, he told the officers, "No, I'm sorry, you got the wrong guy."

My heart almost stopped from the shock. *What? Huh?*

We then made eye contact, he grinned at me again while shaking his head, but this time I recognized it for what it truly was; it wasn't a look of disgust, it was a look of disappointed *love*. He casually turned around and walked back inside and I never saw him again.

I stood there as the officers told me I was free to go. They left, but I still stood there for a good minute trying to process it all. I couldn't believe it, he let me off the hook. I abused the man's trust, I turned my back on him, but he still found me worthy of his compassion. It didn't make any sense, it shouldn't have been that way, and yet somehow it happened, just like how we would describe a miracle.

As I walked home that night, I felt something I hadn't experienced before, it was a peculiar combination of ecstatic joy and being humbled, it was the feeling you could only get when you were given a gift you absolutely did not deserve. *Grace.* After that incident, I vowed to make something of my life with the second chance I was given, and that's exactly what I did.

When we tell people to change their lives out of shame, fear, or pride, we're aiming to transform their exterior, but when we lead people to grace, we're aiming to transform their hearts.

Grace. That's exactly what Jesus Christ did for us. He came into this world to love and serve it, but we demanded for him to be crucified. Despite our betrayal (and continued betrayal whenever we disobey God and prioritize our worldly idols above Him), he still found us worthy of his compassion and endured hell on that cross so that we could have eternal life.

As Christians, we have a couple of options. We can motivate ourselves using the shortcuts of shame, fear or pride, all things that came into this world because of sin and can only lead us further away from God, or, at best, building our own kingdoms, *or* we can look to what once motivated the early Christians, the gospel message that conquered shame, fear and pride, and with true transformation we can now collectively work as the church towards building the kingdom of God with Christ as our leader.

Authenticity

Jumping back to Genesis 3, when Adam and Eve disobeyed God by eating the fruit from the tree of the knowledge of good and evil, their first reaction upon hearing the sound of God walking in the garden was to hide from Him. But God called to Adam, **"Where are you?"** (v.9). When Adam responded that he was hiding because he was naked, God then asked, **"Who told you that you were naked?"** (v.11).

Which raises the question, why would an all-knowing God ask such questions? Surely He already knew the answers? It's the same reason why when my four-year-old son takes an extra lollipop when he's not supposed to, I still ask him if he took it despite his lips and tongue being covered in blue. When we value relationship we also value true and authentic communication. It's no different with God's relationship with us.

God's questioning in the Adam and Eve story, although the result of a disastrous event (the introduction of sin into the world), was the first sign that despite our disobedience, He *still* values us. God does not desire that we should want to hide from Him, but rather that we should walk with Him in the light.

"This is the message we have heard from him and proclaim to you, that God is light, and in him is no darkness at all. If we say we have fellowship with him while we walk in

darkness, we lie and do not practice the truth. But if we walk in the light, as he is in the light, we have fellowship with *one another*, and the blood of Jesus, his Son, purifies us from all sin." (1 John 1:5-7)

This passage from 1 John shows us three things. First, authentic fellowship with God means to walk in the light. Second, only through having authentic fellowship with God can we have authentic fellowship with one another. Finally, walking in the light is what brings us to repentance, thus purifying us of our sins and enabling us to forgive others.

1. To walk in the light means to have authentic fellowship with God.

Last summer, I met up for dinner with a former youth group student of mine, now in his mid-twenties, who was no longer attending church. I remembered that he was once heavily involved in church and seemingly always in a jovial mood, and so I was incredibly curious as to what had happened for him to lose his faith and cheerful spirit.

When I asked him what happened, he began to share some of his life story. His father had instructed him since elementary school that being a good Christian meant he always needed to be happy and **"rejoice in the Lord always"** (Philippians 4:4). And so even when his mother passed away during his early teens, he thought the good Christian thing to do was to suppress his sadness and grief and move on as quickly as possible. He then said something I'll never forget: "David, I never even got to mourn the death of my own mother. What kind of son am I?"

For years, some churches have taught that we can only go before God in the "proper state". Feelings such as anger, sadness, disappointment, fear, grief, or doubt are unacceptable to communicate to God, and therefore those feelings must be suppressed. But at what point does that become exhausting? At what point does it seem like a God who asks us to suppress/ignore our true feelings seem like a God who doesn't actually want an authentic relationship with us? Why should we love a God who does not wish to know our true selves?

God himself displays a wide range of emotions in the Bible. He is alternatively joyful (Isaiah 62:5), grieved (Psalm 78:40), angry (Exodus 4:14), and moved to compassion (Judges 2:18), just to give a few examples. As beings that are made in the image of God (Genesis 1:27), it makes sense that we likewise would have the capacity to feel a wide range of emotions, and therefore, to suppress those emotions is to suppress what God made us to be.

There is perhaps no better example of emotional rawness before God in the Bible than King David, a man who longed after God's own heart. Reading through the Psalms, one is struck by David's unfiltered emotional outcries to God, especially in times of desperation:

"Hasten, O God, to save me; come quickly, Lord, to help me." (Psalm 70:1)

In fact, at no point during its one hundred and fifty chapters do we ever see any of the Psalmists holding back their feelings or emotions in the presence of God. For example:

"Weeping may stay for the night, but rejoicing comes in the morning." (Psalm 30:5)

When reading this text, we so often focus on the rejoicing. And there is theological truth to such words; being with our Father does ultimately lead us to joy and gladness. But the passage also indicates that we are allowed the authentic process of *weeping* prior to the rejoicing.

If I were able to go back in time to that conversation with my former student, I would tell him what I once heard from Rob Reimer, lead pastor of South Shore Community Church in Bridgewater, Massachusetts: "It's okay to not be okay."[6] I would tell him that being a Christian didn't mean that he couldn't mourn his mother's passing. On the contrary, Matthew 5:4 says, **"Blessed are those who mourn, for they will be comforted."**

Even Job, a man of character who feared the Lord, during his time of tremendous suffering was able to be brutally honest with God, saying:

25

"Does it please you to oppress me, to spurn the work of your hands, while you smile on the plans of the wicked?" (Job 10:3)

Yes, Job ultimately does reach the conclusion that he must put his trust in the will of his Maker (Job 42:1-3), but he was also allowed to express his fears and frustrations to God in the process of coming to that conclusion.

During Job's time of suffering, he desired two things: one, for the suffering to cease (obviously), but second, he wanted an audience with God (Job 19:7). He did not feel a need to hide from God while he was experiencing feelings of anger, sadness, disappointment, fear, grief, and doubt. Rather, he was pleading with God to show up in those times. Furthermore, as discussed in more detail later on in this chapter, Job's emotional authenticity eventually led him to a place of *repentance* (Job 42:6), whereas suppressing his feelings may have prevented him from properly understanding the condition of his heart. Because of our incorrect indoctrination, many Christians fear that being emotionally honest in our prayers is a sign of disrespect to God, but the greater disrespect is to pretend to be okay when we are in the presence of the one who knows all.

2. To walk in the light means to have authentic fellowship with one another.

One Saturday night in my early twenties, I went out with a group of close church friends and we got drunk together at a bar in the city. One of my friends' father who was an elder at the church found out and reprimanded a pastor we were all very close to for allowing this to happen under her pastoral watch. This upset me greatly because I strongly felt he was blaming her for his own personal failures as a parent.

A week later, I was at a bar with some buddies and I noticed that very same friend's father drunk at the other end of the bar, so trashed he could barely lift his head. Fully intending to call him out on his blatant hypocrisy, I strolled over and tapped him on the back while his face was planted on the table. He slowly picked up his woozy head and turned around. When he finally recognized who I was after three seconds of processing, his drunken, bloodshot eyes opened wide in panic.

I greeted him properly along with a haughty grin. He then reacted in a manner I did not expect; he aggressively grabbed me by my shirt, pulled my face down so that it was just inches from his mouth (which reeked of alcohol), and frantically pleaded with me, "David, please, please don't tell anyone about this!"

To be frank, I walked away from that man ashamed to be a "Christian." I was ashamed to be associated with this pathetic display of hypocrisy. He reminded me of the Biblical Pharisees, who were so obsessed with looking good on the outside, like **"whitewashed tombs,"** when in reality, something inside of them was dying, like **"bones of the dead and everything unclean"** (Matthew 23:27).

To be fair, I would come to learn a few weeks later that my friend's father was going through quite a bit at the time; he was experiencing financial problems and his brother had just passed away. But after learning this information, what made me sadder than his hypocrisy was the realization that this man was unable to lean on his fellow church members in his time of suffering. He assumed they would be more focused on his outside than concerned for his inside (probably not a wrong assumption), and feared the ensuing shame and judgment from the community. Here was a man who could not be his true self among those in his own church community.

However, Scripture tells us that not only are we called to be in authentic relationship with God, in a gospel culture, we are called to be in authentic relationship with one another.

"But if we walk in the light, as he is in the light, we have fellowship with *one another*, and the blood of Jesus, his Son, purifies us from all sin." (1 John 1:7)

As a church leader, I once feared what people would think about me if I was too honest about my sins and flaws with the congregation. Even some of my closest friends admitted that they could not attend a church where I was pastoring because they simply knew too much about me. And for about a year, I was bothered by the question of whether anyone would actually come to our church if they knew the real me?

Then, during my short time at Alliance Theological Seminary, Dean Ronald Walborn, the most honest pastor I know, confidently assured me, "The only people who get turned off when Christians are too honest are self-righteous Christians. And don't worry about them, there's plenty of churches out there for them. Start a church that's actually for the kinds of people who Jesus spent time ministering to."[7]

In order to have an authentic church, we cannot be concerned about offending self-righteous Christians. Furthermore, when we discourage Christians (whether implicitly or explicitly) from engaging in authentic relationships for the sake of preserving some sort of idealized Christian-church exterior, we are merely creating the appearance of community instead of fostering genuine, Christ-centered relationships. The true gospel cannot be found in such a place.

(That being said, I feel compelled to note that some ways of being transparent within the church community are better than others, and wisdom and discernment are required to know the difference. And while we likewise should not use the need for wisdom and discernment as an excuse for people to hide or suppress their true selves, it is crucial that people are able to find the proper avenues within the community to share their struggles in a way that is ultimately edifying to themselves and to the larger community. For example, it doesn't do much good for the sisters when a man shares with an entire congregation about issues only men can understand and relate to (and vice versa). The man can receive the same healing by disclosing such things exclusively to other brothers.)

In cities like New York where there are so many churches to choose from, it's so easy for Christians to get into the habit of jumping from one church to the next. Our consumer-driven culture teaches us that if a particular church is not exactly meeting our needs, we can just move on to the next in a never-ending search for that perfect church and that perfect community.

Dietrich Bonhoeffer in *Life Together* offers a better solution: don't idealize Christian community at all, shatter the illusion immediately, and allow people to be transparent. It's time we cut the nonsense and stop encouraging Christians to hide their true selves. Let's put it all out in the open, let's bring it to the light.

> **"By sheer grace, God will not permit us to live even for a brief period in a dream world...Only that fellowship which faces such disillusionment, with its unhappy and ugly aspects, begins to be what it should be in God's sight...The sooner this shock of disillusionment comes to an individual and a community the better for both. A community which cannot bear and cannot survive such a crisis, which insists upon keeping its illusion when it should be shattered, permanently loses in that moment the promise of Christian community. Sooner or later it will collapse."[8]**

According to Bonhoeffer, the sooner we realize that there is no perfect church and perfect community, the sooner we can experience the promise of authentic, gospel-centered community. But what is the "promise of Christian community" that Bonhoeffer refers to? This bring me to my final point.

3. Authenticity leads us to repentance and inner healing, as well as the ability to forgive others.

I've never attended an alcohol or drug recovery program, but I hear that the first step to healing is honesty. Thus, such programs typically create non-judgmental environments so that recovering addicts can be honest about themselves and their struggles in front of others. I do, however, attend therapy twice a month, and every time I step into my therapist's office, she reminds me that I am in a safe place where I can honestly express what's going on inside of me (using whatever language necessary for genuine expression). Only in this environment can one experience breakthroughs and allow the healing process to organically take place.

The question I frequently pondered about Christians is this: if church is supposed to be a place of healing, and all other forms of healing begin with being genuine and authentic, why then do

Christians have a reputation for being *inauthentic, hypocritical,* and *judgmental*?[9]

Coming back to Job, an important takeaway from the story of his suffering is that we do not need to hide our feelings from God. However, another important takeaway is that Job's emotional authenticity before God eventually led him to *repentance* (Job 42:6). During Job's suffering, he questioned the goodness and wisdom of God, something he probably never knew he was capable of. And because he was authentic to his feelings, he could properly come to a place of repentance.

While I was a youth group teacher in my early twenties, I was assigned to meet with the high school seniors to help them write their personal testimonies that they would later share with the ministry. As the meetings progressed, I quickly realized that these students had been trained to present a watered-down, sanitized version of themselves at church.

The first student I met with – I'll just call her Lisa – was generally regarded to be the most mature and confident girl in the ministry. She was the one who rallied kids in her grade for get-togethers, organized church events, and made sure those who were neglected were taken care of. If I only looked at her outward appearance, as we so often do, I would've been convinced that she had absolutely no problems in her life.

Lisa calmly sat down in front of my desk and proceeded to share with a cheerful smile, "So, I grew up in church all my life. Thankfully, my parents were both Christians." She paused momentarily to think. "Oh! That's right, and then of course, I met Jesus at a worship night in junior high. It was pretty cool actually, I realized how blessed I was to have him die for me even though I didn't deserve it and all. And since then, I've just been walking with him." She briefly paused again. "And, um, yeah, I guess that's it. Nothing else really." *The end.*

I looked at the few sentences I had scribbled down and asked, "Nothing else?"

"Well, that's all I can think of right now. What can I say? God's been so good to me."

I scratched my head and asked, "What was your life growing up at home like?" I asked because it was something she rarely spoke to anyone at church about. She was usually the shoulder to lean on and the one listening to others vent about their family sorrows.

Her smile quickly vanished. "I'm not gonna share about my life at home," she firmly replied, followed by an uncomfortable chuckle.

It was from her awkward reaction I suspected there was more to her story. I continued, "Can I ask why not?"

Lisa chuckled uneasily again, cleared her throat, and replied, "Cause, I...I just can't."

She started to tremble; I had never seen her this vulnerable before. In fact, I had never seen her vulnerable at all. "Cause they don't wanna hear about it, okay? They...they don't wanna hear about what my dad's like at home, okay? I can't share that. What will they think about me? What will they think about him?" Her father was a well-known leader at the church.

As her shaking increased and the tears started welling up in her eyes, I realized this moment was far more important than the actual task I was given. After all, she would have many opportunities to share about herself while wearing her Sunday mask, but she may only get a few chances to truly be authentic and vulnerable in the house of God. Yes, pushing her to speak to the entire youth group about her father in that context would have probably been inappropriate, but still, she needed to speak to *someone* about it.

I put my pen and paper to the side and gently told her, "Okay, let's forget the testimony, you don't have to share it with the ministry, but please, please, share with someone. It doesn't have to be me, but if you want to share, I will not tell anyone, I give you my word."

Through her tears, she began to share about how her father had put her down all her life, and that she was always self-conscious because of him, never feeling good enough. I realized that this was the underlying reason why she carried the burden of taking care of others. It gave her a sense of self-worth because her father made her feel worthless. Ironically, the most outwardly confident girl in the ministry was actually full of fear and self-loathing on the inside.

When she was finished crying, she earnestly said, "Thank you, I feel so much better now." I was too inexperienced back then to understand how crying her eyes out made her feel better, but in retrospect, I realized she thanked me because I had given her a valuable gift, the gift of authentic Christ-like fellowship, without judgment, that leads to inner healing. I then prayed for her and asked God to help her forgive her father, not for the sake of justifying his actions, but for her own sake, so that *she* could finally be at peace.

The next student that I met with – I'll just call him Sam – was a troubled teenager with a history of anger and violent outbursts. At the time, he had just been expelled from his high school for beating up another student in the school library. He and I were very close, and so I was fully aware of his current situation.

Once he sat down, he coolly shared in his husky voice, "Ya know my story man. My pops left me when I was just a kid, but that's okay, I still managed to make it this far. I taught myself how to fight, how to get them girls. I think I did pretty good for myself despite everythin', ya know? God had my back all along. And my moms raised me, and she did the best job she could. I was able to find Jesus and all that hope 'cause of her. I owe that woman my life, I swear, that's my word." He casually twiddled his thumbs to think some more, but then said, "And that's it, that's my story, my man."

I asked, "What about your father?"

"What 'bout him? There ain't nothin' to share 'bout my pops, I told ya already bro, he wasn't there for me."

Once again, I put my pen and paper to the side and told him to forget the testimony. I wanted him to let it out, right then and there. "Just be honest."

He snickered uneasily. "Why we wastin' our time talkin' 'bout my pops, I already told ya, he ain't have no part of my life." I noticed the pace of his breathing gradually increase. "In fact, my only positive memory of him was when he walked out the door. Ya know, I was relieved and all, 'cause all he used to do was come home drunk and beat me and my moms."

Sam stood up and began to pace back and forth, his fists clenched in anger. I stood up and paced alongside him. Breathing heavily, he said, "Dang, I remember all that man, that wasn't cool. He...he..." He placed his hand on his forehead and stressfully rubbed it a few times. "F***!" he swore at the top of his lungs, unable to contain his emotions any longer. Of course the moment was overwhelming for him. It had to be. Feelings that had been locked away for years were now finally coming to the surface, to the *light.*

Once his breathing had settled, he quickly apologized for his outburst, but I told him that's okay, and encouraged him to keep going. Tears were starting to well up in his eyes. "Right before he left, he beat my moms and dragged her to the door and put her head there, and then he just...he just...slammed the door on her head, like she was nothin' man. Again. And again."

He took a deep breath to try to hold back the tears.

"It's okay," I calmly assured him. "Keep going, bro."

"In fact, if I ever see him again, I'm-ma punch him in the face!"

And then he suddenly broke down crying. We immediately embraced, as hard as we could, as his pain and tears were unleashed onto my shoulder. I let him go at it for a good couple of minutes. It was beautiful. It was *authentic.* Once he stopped, he let go and looked at me with an awkward smile as he wiped his tears with the back of his hand. "Jeez man, I ain't know I was allowed to do that at church."

Therein lies the crux of the problem. We have been so conditioned to present a sanitized version of ourselves at church that we are unable to see the need for healing in our own lives. The longer we live presenting a false version of ourselves to others, the easier it is to believe that the seemingly perfect façade is the true self, and the harder it becomes to see our need for a Savior.

The truth was, Sam probably had no idea just how much anger and resentment he still felt towards his father, and how badly he needed to let it all out. Likewise, Lisa would probably never be able to confront her issues of low self-worth without also confronting the emotional abuse inflicted by her father. That is the promise of authentic Christian community; it allows us to see ourselves in ways that reveal truths we might not otherwise be able to see. It helps us to be truthful about ourselves, especially when we have difficulty admitting what we have to be truthful about.

Teaching people that they must present a façade at church is not the workings of a God who is a God of truth (1 John 1:5-6). Rather, it is the working of Satan who is the father of lies (John 8:44). And yes, as Christians we need to be set apart (Ephesians 5:11), meaning we are called to act and behave differently than non-Christians. However, being set apart is not simply a matter of outward appearance, nor is it about behavior modification. A Christ-like heart and attitude can only come through *inner* transformation through the power of the gospel. Recognizing God's grace in our lives is what stirs in us a deep desire for godly living, and an essential component of that transformation is being able to speak truthfully to one another.

"You were taught, with regard to your former way of life, to put off your old self, which is being corrupted by its deceitful desires; to be made new in the attitude of your minds; and to put on the new self, created to be like God in true righteousness and holiness. *Therefore, each of you must put off falsehood and speak truthfully to your neighbor, for we are all members of one body.***" (1 Corinthians 4:22-24)**

Jean Vanier writes in *From Brokenness to Community*, "To be in communion means to be with someone and to discover that we actually belong together. Communion means accepting people *just as they are*, with all their limits and inner pain, but also with their gifts and their beauty and capacity to grow: to see the beauty inside all of the pain."[10]

This is just as true for pastors and church leaders as it is for laypersons in the church. What Vanier realized was that church leaders were pretending to be okay when facing their congregations, but in reality, their personal lives were a mess, often manifesting in ugly neglect and abuse towards their families. He writes, "Pastors and church leaders who aren't daily admitting that they are a mess and rather desperate in need of daily forgiving and transforming grace become very skilled self-swindlers"[11]

Pastors, church leaders, lay-Christians, *everyone* has junk and brokenness inside. If we are not confessing it regularly, we simply end up fooling ourselves and others. An absence of authentic relationships (both with God and with others) often results in a lack of genuine repentance (Matthew 3:8) and a failure to allow God to become our ultimate healer (Psalm 147:3).

To be sure, being authentic about our brokenness (first to God, and then to others) is a difficult task, but the Bible is clear that Jesus came for the broken. Therefore, it is far more important that Christians are being honest about our brokenness and seeking repentance and healing regularly, than to put on a brave face and avoid showing any real emotion. If that shatters others' image of us, good. Even the Apostle Paul labels himself a broken man, the worst of sinners, but in doing so, he points the way to Jesus Christ who came to save the sinners (1 Timothy 1:15).

A couple of summers ago, a man tapped me on my shoulder in a parking lot while I was strapping my son into his car seat and politely asked, "Excuse me, do you think I can quickly get something from my car? You're blocking my door."

Feeling disrespected, I then swung around to face him and angrily shouted, "WAIT YOUR TURN!" He quickly backed off after seeing my harsh reaction while I turned around to finish strapping my son in.

While driving home, I felt ashamed that I had overreacted, especially since I was a father, a Christian, and a pastor. Lashing out at strangers was not a frequent occurrence in that period of my life. But as I was questioning why I would get so angry over something so trivial, I realized that I still had so much bitterness and anger inside me; I just had stored it away so deep I forgot it existed.

Suddenly, while I was still driving, I had these flashbacks dating back to my childhood. I remembered when I was in the fourth grade and the teacher asked everyone who the strongest kid in the class was and they all shouted in unison, "ROGER!" (Roger was a fourth-grade kid that looked like he was made out of bricks.) She then asked who they thought the weakest kid in the class was, and they all (*all* thirty-two other kids) shouted at once, "DAVID!" I sat low in my chair for the remainder of that morning, wishing I no longer existed.

I remembered being the only Asian kid in my neighborhood in the sixth grade and walking home from school when I got jumped by a mob of kids as they struck me from the back, threw me to the ground, and proceeded to kick and stomp me. They then reached into my pockets, stole my keys and money, and shouted racist remarks such as, "Go back to your country you stupid chink!" I recalled that helpless feeling of being so vulnerable as I cried while shriveled up beneath their callous laughter.

I remembered in high school, I was waiting to get my lunch and a bigger bully shoved me out of the line using brute force and shouted, "MOVE, LOSER!" He and his groups of friends then laughed at me while they gave each other high fives.

As these memories, which had been held so tightly for so many years were finally unleashed, I realized that just because they were buried away didn't mean I had forgiven those people. Thus, when I lashed out at the man in the parking lot, I wasn't necessarily lashing out at just him, I was lashing out at those who had hurt me in my past. And so, what I was actually telling the man was that I was no longer the weakest kid in the class, that I was no longer the Asian kid who would stay down on the ground, that I was no longer the loser who could be bullied out of the lunch line, and so to all you jerks who hurt me, "WAIT YOUR TURN!"

It's peculiar that something that occurred while I was in elementary school still affected me in my thirties. In fact, once, after I gave a message on authenticity, an African American woman in her late sixties approached me and opened up about how *fifty* years ago, when she was in high school, she was regularly teased by the other African American girls in her neighborhood because she was light-skinned. She confessed that she had never given it much thought since then, but she now realized it still controlled her and contributed significantly to her social anxiety. I was able to pray for her afterwards, but had she not been truthful about her pain, she would never have understood that she still needed healing after all these years.

Of course, seasoned Christians are generally aware that Scripture calls us to forgive:

"For if you forgive other people when they sin against you, your heavenly Father will also forgive you." (Matthew 6:14)

Unfortunately, many of us confuse forgiveness with simply moving on with our lives, but in actuality, the two don't always go hand in hand. While many of us have been taught since childhood that moving on is the strong way, the truth is that it takes far more strength and courage to confront our feelings and truly forgive those who have hurt us in the past.

I have good friend named George, a big strong muscular guy with a tough exterior. One time at church, in our mid-twenties, an older woman that we knew sat with us for lunch, and out of the blue, she told him that he needed to forgive his father for physically abusing him as a child and leaving his family.

At first, George laughed it off, and casually replied, "No, that's okay, I don't need to forgive my father. I've already forgotten all about him and moved on."

But she persistently insisted, "No, you *must* forgive him."

He laughed again. "If I forgive him, that means I'm acknowledging what he did to me and my family was okay, but it wasn't okay, so I ain't gonna forgive him. But instead, I'm gonna learn from his mistakes. I'm gonna become a better man and father than he ever was."

She continued, "George, you will never become a better man and father until you forgive him because he will always be a part of you."

I could sense my buddy starting to get irritated, as he adamantly shook his head and insisted, "No, no, he's not a part of me, that man has nothing to do with me."

They went back and forth for a bit and then the discussion finally came to a close because we had to go. But a couple of days later, he and I talked in private, and he realized from getting so worked up during the prior conversation that his father did, in fact, still have a huge impact on his life. George was wrong in the sense that forgiveness doesn't mean telling someone what he/she did to us was okay, but instead we forgive so that our *own* inner healing process can begin.

We would so often rather move on than acknowledge that somebody hurt us because forgiving others, itself, hurts. There is a cost to forgiving, and we don't want to pay that cost.

But the cost for the forgiveness of our sins was the sacrifice of Jesus Christ, and that cost hurt immensely. Just imagine if God decided to merely move on instead of paying that cost, none of us would be deemed worthy of entering the kingdom of heaven (Romans 3:23). Yes, of course there is peace in forgiveness, but we primarily face the truth, forgive, and pay that cost because the gospel tells us that Christ first paid the cost for us.

Community

While I was in college, I ran into a former church friend of mine who I hadn't seen for a few years. When I asked her why I hadn't seen her, she replied, "Oh, I don't go to church anymore. But, it doesn't mean I'm not a Christian! I just thought one day, what's the point of going through the hassle of getting there? Now I can just wake up on Sundays whenever I want and listen to a better sermon online. In fact, I probably get more out it."

This conversation was back in 2001, when sermons had just begun to hit the internet. Today, the options are seemingly limitless, which likely increases the number of those who echo the above sentiment, the same sentiment the pop star Justin Bieber once expressed in an interview with *Complex Magazine*: "You don't need to go to church to be a Christian. If you go to Taco Bell that doesn't make you a taco."[12]

But such statements raise a curious question: "Is church, in fact, an essential element to Christian life?" After all, if the primary purpose of attending church is to be entertained or to sit through some sort of religious self-help program, then it's possible that merely listening to our favorite celebrity preachers online may fill that void. But when we look at the Biblical definition of church, it is less about a one-day-a-week experience tailor-made to make us feel good or to get our weekly spiritual fix in, and more about being a part of something special; a family, a *body*.

"And God placed all things under his feet and appointed him to be head over everything for the church, *which is his body*, the fullness of him who fills everything in every way." (Ephesians 1:22-23)

We see from the Biblical definition above that church was not meant to be something we simply attend, such as going to a movie. Neither is church a place or a building. It's the body of Christ; it's who we are and who we should be at all times. To be fair, many church-going Christians frequently contradict this definition when we treat our Sunday worship experience differently from the remainder of our week. With such inconsistency, we cloud the truth that we are, in fact, the church, whether we are inside a building used for collective Christian worship or in our homes, schools, workplaces, or wherever else.

As a Christian, it would be logically inconsistent to place one's faith in the claims of the Bible and then simply ignore the 100+ Bible verses that emphasize the importance of Christian community.

"And let us consider how we may spur one another on toward love and good deeds, not giving up meeting together, as some are in the habit of doing." (Hebrews 10:24)

"How good and pleasant it is when God's people live together in unity!" (Psalm 133:1)

Furthermore, the Epistles (the letters in the New Testament) provide evidence of the historical significance of Christian community (the family, the *body*) during the first century, not just within the churches themselves, but also between the authors and those receiving the letters:

"Night and day we pray most earnestly that we may see you again and supply what is lacking in your faith." (1 Thessalonians 3:10)

There is no doubt when we read Scripture that community is vital to Christian life. Here are some practical reasons why it is essential to our Christian walk.

1. The quality of our Christian community is our most effective evangelistic tool.

Against all odds and logic, and despite Christians being persecuted by both Jewish authorities and the Roman government prior to the Constantine settlement, Christianity still grew at an astonishing rate during the first century A.D.[13] It was a movement so dissimilar to anything prior to its time that it piqued many people's intrigue and curiosity.

For instance, Jews, who had always separated themselves from Gentiles (non-Jews) for centuries, viewing them to be unclean and sometimes even barbaric, suddenly began to send missionaries into Antioch and other non-Jewish cities for the primary purpose of ministering to Gentiles (Galatians 2:11-12). Furthermore, first century Christians were radically generous with their money and belongings, selling their property and pooling together their possessions to distribute to the poor (Acts 2:44:44). Barriers between people of different races, genders, and socioeconomic status were being removed (Galatians 3:28), and people with little to no standing in society such as slaves and women were told that they were now *equals* with others in Christ Jesus (Galatians 3:28). The only conclusion that people could come up with was that there must have been some divine spark that ignited this movement. No mortal man could inspire so many to act this way. Rodney Stark describes this phenomenon as follows:

"Christianity did not grow because of miracle working in the marketplaces (although there may have been much of that going on), or because Constantine said it should, or even because the martyrs gave it such credibility. It grew because Christians constituted an *intense community*, able to generate the 'invincible obstinacy' that so offended the younger Pliny but yielded immense religious rewards. And the primary means of its growth was through the united and motivated

40

efforts of the growing numbers of Christian believers, who invited their friends, relatives, and neighbors to share the 'good news.'"[14]

The *united* and *passionate* nature of the first-century Christian community organically drew people towards the early church, and the gospel message transformed them so that they remained part of the church. It is not simply our gatherings as a congregation that will capture the attention of non-believers, but it is the *way* in which we gather. Our love must come from the direct overflow of Christ's love in us. A Christian community that shows itself to be uniquely selfless, united, and humble in the quality of our community will draw others towards the love of Christ.

David Swaim, lead pastor of High Rock, a network of churches in the greater area of Boston, once discovered that a local soup kitchen was on the cusp of being shut down due to a lack of funding.[15] High Rock answered the call and organized a successful Christmas concert and donated all of the proceeds to the soup kitchen so that they were able to remain open.[16] High Rock continued to do this, year after year, until ironically, the church was asked to stop by the soup kitchen because they were receiving too much money.

The generosity of High Rock caught the attention of the city, and their story was eventually printed in the Boston Globe.[17] Even the mayor of Boston gave David a phone call to thank him for the impact the church was making. Simply put, High Rock was loving others with no strings attached, and any community that loves without contingencies will undoubtedly blow the minds of the people of this world.

But of course, to love without contingencies can be a struggle. It goes against our sinful natures. The church where I served as a youth pastor had an attractive gym facility, which was a draw for teenagers in the neighborhood. Many of these teens would come on Fridays before our evening youth service to play basketball or soccer. However, one day I informed them that they could only use our facility if they attended our service afterwards. And some of them did, and thus, it turned out to be somewhat of an effective evangelism tool.

But I frequently wondered, what about those that didn't want to come to service? Were they not worthy of my love and generosity as well?

In retrospect, perhaps a better idea would've been to make a separate day in which all the neighborhood kids could come to the gym and play, regardless of if they attended our service, so that they would know that we loved them just for the sake of loving of them.

Yes, evangelism is necessary (Matthew 28:19) and should be an integral part of the DNA of churches and Christians. And yes, we need programs that are specifically designed for expanding God's kingdom, but even above such things our greatest calling for this world is to simply *love* without any conditions or strings attached (Mark 12:31).

Furthermore, there is a strong temptation for churches to operate using a cost-benefit analysis like secular businesses. Whether consciously or subconsciously, we tend to invest more in ministries that draw in newcomers and/or produce larger financial gains. After all, it is easier to invest, serve, and love when we are able to tangibly see the results because we can then point to the numbers as evidence of "God's movement." But as David Swaim once said in a sermon when explaining the difficulty of adopting eleven children (yes, not a typo, *eleven*), many of whom had never learned to express gratitude or appreciation, even to a man who had given his life to raising them, "Our love for others in Christ will *never* go to waste."[18]

When Christ washed the feet of his disciples, this was a rather shocking occurrence since such work was reserved for slaves, the lowest members of households, or anyone who could not contribute anything of value to society, so much so that the Apostle Peter adamantly refused to let it happen at first (John 13:1-8). And yet, Christ calls us to do the same for one another (John 13:14).

It seems impossible that anyone would be attracted to a religion that instructs you to serve others in the same selfless and self-denying manner as Christ (John 13:12-15). For us to have the hearts of servants, or the status of slave or the lowest members of a household is completely countercultural to our modern sensibilities (and to our sinful natures). Why would people voluntarily place this burden in their lives?

And yet, such selfless behavior was one of the primary reasons that large numbers of people were attracted to the first century church. But why? Why does that intrigue anyone? Why did people want to know more about High Rock when news spread of their selfless acts and donations towards the soup kitchen? At the end of the day, they wanted to know what the driving force was behind these selfless acts.

When Peter vehemently refused to have his feet washed, Christ surprisingly responded in a fairly harsh and severe manner, saying, **"Unless I wash you, you have no part with me"** (John 13:8). Common sense tells us that Peter should have been the one to wash his master's feet, not the other way around. But Jesus was making the point that he *must* be our servant first before we can serve others. If he is not, we can never love just for the sake of loving; we will always be self-seeking in our acts of service, i.e., our motivation for loving others will always partly be about earning God's love.

I once counseled a young man who was struggling in his faith. He explained to me that he had been serving faithfully at his church and praying every day. He had even read the Bible in its entirety, and yet there was still something missing in his heart. He didn't feel moved or satisfied–in fact, he felt rather lifeless inside.

I eventually asked him the very simple question, "Tell me, who is God in your life?"

He confidently answered, "He is my father, master, creator, designer, and planner."

I then asked, "How do you interact with Him?"

"Well, I mostly wait for Him to tell me what to do."

"And that's it?"

"Yeah, that's it."

And right then and there, I was able to locate the problem. He had embraced God as the almighty who sits on high, but never embraced Him as the one who came low and humbly served him. All of the young man's characterizations of God were theologically true, God is our father, master, creator, designer and planner, but until He comes in the form of Christ and serves us, none of us will ever truly be moved by the gospel.

2. Community reveals to us a larger part of the gospel.

I won't get into this too much here since we'll be going more in depth when discussing the value of diversity, but one of the benefits of being in community is that it allows us to understand the gospel in new ways. To illustrate, a few years back, while I was going through a spiritually dry period in my life, a friend of mine named John told a touching story about a theological conversation he had overheard between his two daughters. The one who was five was telling the one who was three about Jesus' sacrifice and how that creates "teams," and the younger sister replied, "Oh! I get it now! So if I'm good, I'm on God's team and if I'm bad, I'm on Satan's team!" John was so proud of his little girl; she was learning to associate good with God and bad with Satan. But much to his surprise, the older sister then corrected her, "No, that's not true. Because of Jesus, *even if* you are bad you'll be on God's team, you'll always be on God's team, you'll never leave God's team."

As I heard the story, I cried out of overwhelming emotion, because I had learned something so valuable from a girl who was only five years old; that "because of Jesus I will always be on God's team." You see, that little girl taught me something precious about the gospel that I could not have picked up from an adult. These words, if spoken by anyone my age, would not have had the same impact simply because it would not have been told with the same childlike faith, the same innocence and security in Jesus.

In the same way, people of different races, cultures, socioeconomic status, gender, and life experiences from ourselves relate to the gospel in ways that we are not able to. Christian community allows us to learn from one another things about the gospel we may not otherwise have been able to perceive or notice. Without Christian community, it would be like standing in front of a gigantic cube that's painted differently with various artwork on all sides and only being able to see the side that's presented directly in front of us.

At the risk of sounding cliché, if you were crossing a street with a car coming directly at you and someone were to dash over and shove you out of the way to spare your life in exchange for theirs, wouldn't you want to know who this person was? Wouldn't you want to learn as much about this person as possible? And yet, the reward of Christ's sacrifice was so much greater than this hypothetical. After all, we are all going to die one day, and so saving someone's life isn't actually saving their life; it's merely extending it. Christ's sacrifice doesn't just save our lives, it saves our souls. Thus, we wish to honor him by getting to know as much of him as possible, and not just the side of the cube that directly faces us, but to seek him in his *entirety*.

3. Community is the most effective way to live a Godly life.

When God created the heavens and the earth, He declared everything to be "good," with one exception: God said it was not good for man to be alone (Genesis 2:18). God has always been a God of community, as evidenced by the triune nature of God made manifest in the Holy Trinity, and Man, who was created in the image of God, was likewise not meant to be alone (Matthew 28:19).

Therefore, by design and by our nature, human beings are not meant to do life alone. The best Biblical example of this is, of course, Christ, who came to earth in the form of man to model for us godly living and decided that it was essential to surround himself with twelve best friends (Matthew 4:18-22). Those who claim they can merely listen to sermons online to build their relationship with God and do not need to develop further Christian community are basically claiming they possess the ability to do something that even Christ acknowledged it would not be in his best interests to do.

During my time in youth ministry, I came across hundreds of students who claimed to be touched by Jesus, but it was usually easy to differentiate between those who were genuine about cultivating their Christian walk and those who weren't quite motivated enough to let anything deeper develop from their experience. The ones who immediately sought after Christian community continued to deepen their faith, and those who didn't simply returned to their lives as if nothing had happened. Which tells me at the very least, it is easier to live a Christian life when surrounded by Christian community than not. Now if this is the case, and the gospel moves us to desire a loving relationship with Jesus (1 John 5:1), why would we not select the easier route of getting there?

Furthermore, the gospel leads us towards a desire to live out a *transformative godly life*:

45

"For the grace of God has appeared that offers salvation to all people. It teaches us to say 'No' to ungodliness and worldly passions, and to live self-controlled, upright and godly lives in this present age." (Titus 2:11-12)

Some years back, I knew a close group of guy friends who were getting belligerently drunk together a couple of times a week, often leading to detrimental results. Eventually, they collectively decided they were heading down the wrong path and switched their passions over to serving in church, and just like that, the belligerent drunken nights were no longer a part of their routine. They became heavily involved in the Lord's work, some as youth leaders, one as a college group coordinator, and another became a pastor. The point of this story is that it is far easier for people to shift from one lifestyle to another when doing it together.

In a world where temptation is constantly at our doorstep, we are called to be a new creation (2 Corinthians 5:17). However, it is not easy to simply shift from **"ungodliness and worldly passions"** to an **"upright and godly life"** (Titus 2:12), and to try to do it alone is even more difficult. That is why Christian community is essential.

Moreover, godly living is a road marked with all kinds of persecution:

"In fact, everyone who wants to live a godly life in Christ Jesus will be persecuted." (2 Timothy 3:12)

When we generally think of Christians being persecuted, we tend to picture martyrs and underground missionaries, or perhaps to a lesser degree, those of us who get mocked at our schools or workplaces for our faith. While many of us may never experience these more blatant forms of persecution during our lifetime, the reality is that a more subtle form of persecution is all around us.

For example, a few years after I had given my life to Christ, some old high school guy friends of mine that I hadn't seen for years called me out to a mini-reunion with them at a bar. I went over and grabbed a drink with the old crew, but as I sat there listening to story after story about their sexual conquests, I realized our core values were no longer in sync. It wasn't that a lifestyle of sexual conquests wasn't desirable for me at the time (the temptation was real), but even greater was my desire to live a godly lifestyle. Therefore, as I sat there in the midst of them, I realized that I was an underdog in this world. Christians are underdogs; we are meant to be. After all, Christ himself was an underdog. For the most part, our desires do not align with those of the world (they shouldn't), and when we are living in this world, we will constantly be bombarded with messages that are counter to our values and beliefs.

Thus, when the first century church underwent such persecution as underdogs, they responded with **"glad and sincere hearts"** (Acts 2:46), by banding together and breaking bread with one another. This tells us that when Jesus enters one's life, to live a godly life is not a chore, but instead it is a joyful desire that swirls around in our renewed hearts. As such, we long to celebrate and share that same desire with others who are of the same mind, heart, and soul.

4. Christian community allows us to share common life experiences, passions, and goals.

Some years back, Jany and I watched the foreign film *Sin Nombre*, directed by Cary Jôji Fukunaga.[19] The fictional film was about the real Mexican gang Mara Salvatrucha (a/k/a MS-13). What fascinated me, more than the story itself, was the MS-13 members' undying loyalty to the gang, to the extent that when a complete stranger with the requisite gang tattoos would walk onto their turf, they would clothe, feed, and house him, and basically treat him like a brother.[20] But they wouldn't really know the slightest thing about the character or personality of this person beforehand. He could be the most annoying being in the world for all they knew, but it didn't matter as long as he had the MS-13 gang tattoos.

At first thought, that seemed a bit illogical. But after some evaluating, I realized it wasn't the tattoos themselves that gained one entry into the gang; it was what they signified, the common experience of being a member of MS-13. When someone had the requisite tattoos, you instantly knew he did something crazy to be initiated into the gang

47

in order to obtain them. In other words, you shared a common life experience with this person that probably involved killing somebody. And now you shared a common passion and goal, which was to represent the gang through life and death.

Community (and friendship) is based on the commonality we share in our life experiences, passions, and goals. Community would have no purpose otherwise.

To further explain, one night, I was sitting around with three of my best friends listening to one of them vent about how his father had greatly disappointed him.

Then suddenly, I impulsively interrupted, "Hey! At least your dad's around, my dad left for Korea when I was just a kid!"

Then my other friend jumped in, "Hey! At least you knew your dad at all! I never really got to know my father, he split before I was even born!"

Then another joined in, "Hey! You guys are lucky, anything's better than my dad, my dad's the worst human being alive! I wish I never knew this guy!"

And suddenly, we got into this huge shouting match about who had the worst situation with their dads, and I realized while driving home afterwards that I was naturally drawn to people who came from dysfunctional or broken families like myself. *Common life experience.*

Furthermore, when I was in sixth grade growing up in Woodside, Queens, I would routinely walk to the comic book store a couple of blocks from my house. One afternoon, I noticed a few kids looking at vintage Star Wars figurines from 1977. I couldn't believe it, they were Star Wars fans, just like myself. Next thing I knew, we were sitting on milk crates in the garage of one of the kid's homes doing Star Wars trivia and arguing about who was most suited to be the Han Solo of the group. We shared a *common passion*, Star Wars, and a *common goal*, to be the geekiest kids in our neighborhood.

When we ask people to reach out to others in church, a typical response we may get is that they don't have anything in common. However, this cannot be true in the family of Jesus Christ, for we all share the same life experience–that we were once dead in our sins, but because of Christ's sacrifice, we now have eternal life. We share the same passion, to love Jesus and others as a result of the grace he has shown us. We share the same goal, to tell others the good news, that Christ has conquered sin and given us freedom.

When we read about the first century church in the book of Acts, we notice some rather interesting behavior from these people who historically had nothing in common:

"They devoted themselves to the apostles' teaching and to fellowship, to the breaking of bread and to prayer. Everyone was filled with awe at the many wonders and signs performed by the apostles. All the believers were together and had everything in common. They sold property and possessions to give to anyone who had need. Every day they continued to meet together in the temple courts. They broke bread in their homes and ate together with glad and sincere hearts, praising God and enjoying the favor of all the people. And the Lord added to their number daily those who were being saved." (Acts 2:42-47)

Interestingly, in this group you had a mix of the powerful and the powerless, the successful and the failures, the rich and the poor, meeting together every day in the temple courts for worship and fellowship, drawing in more and more people daily (v. 46-47). What would cause such a thing? What would make the powerful and the powerless break bread with one another (v. 46)? What would make the successful and the failures do discipleship together (v. 42)? What would have the rich pool their material belongings together so that they could give it to the poor (v. 44-45)? It is because they realized power, success, and material wealth were only temporary gains, but the kingdom of heaven was an eternal investment (Luke 6:38). Their true power, success, and wealth came when Christ made himself powerless, a failure, and poor as he was unjustly tortured, mocked, and placed on that cross. Therefore, despite their differences, they knew that if they had Jesus in common, they truly had *everything* in common.

In order for us to have everything in common, we must become less and allow Christ to become more. It must be less about our differences and more about how he has graciously washed all of our feet (John 13:8).

If a gang could come to accept one another as family over a commonality that involves killing, then how much more should we love and accept each other as Christians over a commonality that involves *saving*. Christian community should not be a legalistic chore that we must reluctantly fulfill, but instead it allows us to worship, fellowship, and celebrate with those with whom we have everything in common.

Being Missional

In high school and college, I used to attend various retreats and worship nights where guest speakers would facilitate specific altar calls for those who felt called to be a pastor or missionary. We tend to treat these callings like they're special, and don't get me wrong, they are, but so are the callings of the lay people. In fact, the gospel did not primarily spread because people answered "special" callings, but rather, *everyone* who followed Christ, in various places, positions, and offices played a role in the spreading of the good news. In other words, there was not a single Christian without a special calling.

"Those who had been scattered preached the word wherever they went." (Acts 8:4)

"Nevertheless, each person should live as a believer in whatever situation the Lord has assigned to them, just as God has called them." (1 Corinthians 7:17)

All believers have callings. We're called to neighborhoods, cities, specific people, workplaces, schools, and homes. We see in the Bible one of the first examples of a calling to a specific region when God called Abraham to leave his home:

"I will make you into a great nation, and I will bless you; I will make your name great, and you will be a blessing." (Genesis 12:2)

We so often focus on the blessings narrative when discussing the Abraham story (the descendants, the "great nation," the making of his "name great") but what we don't talk about as much are the reasons for the blessings. At the end of the passage above, God tells Abraham, **"You will be a blessing"** (Genesis 12:2). There is such rich theological truth to those words. God blesses us so that we can then be a blessing towards others. We are not called to simply sit back and enjoy the ride. We are called to be active members of our congregations, both inside the church walls *and* outside. We are called to be *missional*, a term Dr. Eric Mason of Epiphany Fellowship Church in Philadelphia, PA, defines as, "The identity of the people of God by which we live out our nature as God's ambassadors to the world in which we join Him in His effort to reach people."[21]

Here are five things to keep in mind when being a missional church community:

1. We must be mindful of non-Christians whenever we gather as a church community.

During my church planting training with Redeemer City to City, Timothy Keller and Robert Guerrero frequently emphasized the importance of preaching to *both* believers and non-believers at the same time. (For those who have listened to Keller's messages, you know he absolutely excels at this.) For example, in today's postmodern (or post-Christian) society, most people who do not grow up with church culture are ill-equipped to understand basic church terminology (or as some of us playfully call it, Christian-ese).[22] However, preachers frequently use words such as "sin" and even "gospel" in their messages without any explanation, assuming everyone listening has at least a rudimentary understanding of what they mean. But one of the primary goals within the missional church should be to be as *inclusive* as possible.[23] If preachers, small group leaders, or congregation members are throwing around Christian terminology without explanation in the presence of non-believers, the message we give them is that you must meet us where we're at, rather than the truth that the gospel meets you where you're at.

And furthermore, we need to be cognizant and understanding of the fact that non-believers or baby (new) Christians who did not grow up in the church are unfamiliar with the same Christian traditions that we're used to being immersed in. For example, one Sunday at a local church I grew up in, we had a newcomer non-Christian come by who was using swear words among the adults during fellowship time after service. Now putting aside theological opinions on swearing, our congregation frowned upon the usage of such words inside our church building. So when this newcomer who was unfamiliar with this culture was walking around uttering four letter words in the fellowship hall, people began to stare at him like he was an alien from outer space. Instead of accepting him as part of the community "as is," as a truly missional church would do, we were judging him unfairly according to social norms that were foreign to him, and therefore failing to be inclusive.

When we act standoffish or hostile towards those who do not meet our behavioral or cultural standards, we send the message that, "you must change before we can accept you." As we see in Scripture, Christ never utters such a message. His message is always to meet people where they are at, and any form of subsequent transformation in their lives are a result of the power of this encounter.

2. Being missional encourages non-Christians to come as they are.

My wife Jany and I once invited a young woman over to our house for dinner. During the course of our conversation, she explained that she had been judged at every church she'd ever stepped inside. And yes, she admitted to not being as outwardly religious or moral as other churchgoers, but she sincerely asked us, "I thought churches were supposed to accept sinners? They always say that, don't they? But then why do I always feel shunned every time I attend?"

Sadly, churches are generally now seen as a place for the hypocritical (fake) and judgmental rather than a place for those Jesus spent his ministry reaching out to – sinners, outsiders, the irreligious and those living in the margins of society – thus hindering the spread of the gospel. As Timothy Keller puts it in *The Prodigal God*:

> **"Jesus's teaching consistently attracted the irreligious while offending the Bible-believing, religious people of his day. However, in the main, our churches today do not have this effect. The kind of outsiders Jesus attracted are not attracted to contemporary churches, even our most avant-garde ones. We tend to draw conservative, buttoned-down, moralistic people. The licentious and liberated or the broken and marginal avoid church. That can only mean one thing. If the preaching of our ministers and the practice of our parishioners do not have the same effect on people that Jesus had, then we must not be declaring the same message that Jesus did."[24]**

I strongly believe the primary reason churches today are having difficulty drawing in the "licentious and liberated or the broken and marginal" is because we tend to care more about the outside of people than the inside. This truth was made real to me when listening to the personal testimony of Finney Varughese, lead pastor of Hope Church Long Island.

While growing up in Jamaica, Queens, Finney had a best friend named Faizel. When the two reached high school, their paths diverged. Finney found Jesus and Faizel became a gang leader. But they remained close, like brothers, and Finney spent many years trying to convince Faizel to come to church. Unfortunately, he was unsuccessful with each attempt.

Then one day, Finney heard of a worship night at a local church, and when he went through his usual routine of inviting Faizel to join, much to his surprise, he agreed to attend this time. Finney was ecstatic at the opportunity; he had been praying and looking forward to this day for so long.

When the two arrived at the church, an older man standing at the front door looked at Faizel and sternly called out, "Hey you!" The two friends glanced at one another in confusion, unsure exactly who he was speaking to. The man then pointed directly at Faizel and spoke harshly, "You, I'm talking to *you*. You can't come in here dressed like that." Faizel was wearing a backwards cap, tank top and baggy jeans. The man reiterated, "I *said*, you can't come in here like that."

The two turned around and left. Afterwards, Finney apologized to his friend multiple times on behalf of Christians, but the damage had been done. Faizel never returned to church, and unfortunately, not too long afterwards he was killed in an automobile accident.

Finney was devastated by his friend's death; it is a story he cannot share till this day without tears flowing from his eyes. He told me that he frequently thinks about the time he brought Faizel to that church, how things might've turned out differently if the man had just allowed them inside. It makes him angry and sad that some people just don't understand how much Jesus loves the Faizels of this world and desires for them to be accepted into his family. We cannot demand for people to change before we accept them. We must first accept them where they are, for this is the way in which Christ ran his ministry.

In Luke 19:1-10, Zacchaeus, a tax collector, a man who cheated others out of their money for his own personal gain, climbs a tree in order to see Jesus. And Jesus spots him and invites himself over to Zacchaeus' house, much to the chagrin of the crowd who detests the tax collector (understandably so). But Zacchaeus is so moved by this encounter that he agrees to sell half his possessions to the poor and pay back anyone he had cheated four times the amount (v. 8). Jesus never makes it a contingency that Zacchaeus has to do this first before he accepts him or has a relationship with him. Jesus meets him exactly where he is at. Zacchaeus' transformation from a robber into one who is radically generous with his money and possessions is a direct result of his moving encounter with Christ. Imagine if Zacchaeus is never allowed to meet Jesus because of who he is or how he looks?

I get that as Christians, we want people to change. But we must be careful not to demand behavior modification or other merely exterior changes as a condition of acceptance into the family of God. Imagine if the Apostle Paul, when he was still called Saul, was told he needed to change his ways before he could have his encounter with Christ on the road to Damascus (Acts 9:1-19). Surely a man who was so obstinate and fixated on the persecution of Christians would never have agreed to such terms. But God, in his mercy, meets Saul on the road to Damascus, and it is this encounter that transforms a religious zealot who persecuted Christians to one of most important, if not the most important, gospel evangelists of the early church. Likewise, it is Zacchaeus' encounter with Christ that causes him to change his ways. In a missional church, transformation happens organically as Christ reaches the hearts of the lost. No prior behavior modification is required. The truth is we are *all* fragmented, broken versions of our complete self, which we will only be able to see fully in heaven (1 Corinthians 13:12).

3. Being missional requires us to seek the peace of the city/neighborhood.

In the same message where David Swaim spoke of High Rock's impact on the local soup kitchen in Boston, he also encouraged us to be churches that were for the neighborhoods and cities that we were in. After all, even when the Israelites were held captive by the Babylonians, God did not tell them to spit on their temporary situation, but rather to seek the *shalom* of the city (Jeremiah 29:5-7); to seek its peace and prosperity through advocating for justice, reconciliation, feeding the poor, looking after the environment, engaging in society through politics, being servants for the city, etc. (all such things were encompassed in the Jewish word *shalom*–it was the perfect weaving together of God and His people).

One of my seminary professors once shared with me his disappointment of his sole experience of stepping inside a church in South Korea. He said to me, "David, I was so excited to see all the Korean culture, and as soon as service started, the choir came out wearing the exact same robes that white churches wear, and then they started singing the exact same songs we sing, only translated into Korean. What's that all about?"

The answer lies in the fact that when European and American missionaries initially went into certain areas in Asia and South America, they did not do a lot of listening or learning about the local people's cultures. Instead, they simply told them to do church a certain way, *their* way. This resulted in a lot of initial tension and distrust between the locals and the missionaries.

When we place a church in a specific neighborhood or city and we are unwilling to listen to the local people, we are sending the message that we don't truly care about them or their experiences. How then can we ever be their advocates or seek the shalom of their city if they don't believe we care?

Before planting a church in eastern Queens, I spent a lot of time just listening to the stories of its residents. I heard all kinds of stories; stories about a lack of trust towards the local church, stories of the positive/negative impact churches have had on specific areas and its people, I even heard stories about the history of the local pizzerias. My willingness to listen created a sense of trust, and those I encountered understood that I was not coming in to change their culture, but rather to learn about it so that I may preach the gospel of Jesus in a manner that was relatable to them.

Don't get me wrong, I am not saying we must always do whatever the locals tell us to do, or ever compromise our mission goals and fundamental beliefs, for the one thing God does not instruct the Israelites to do during their Babylonian captivity is to become like the Babylonians (Jeremiah 29:1-23). But it must be evident through our actions that we are *for* them, and as David Swaim mentions in his message about High Rock's impact on Boston, "We must pray for the humility to *listen* to them."[25]

When looking at the churches spread across the city in the Hope Church NYC network for example, we do not expect all the churches to look or operate in the same way. Instead, there must be deliberate attempts of adapting (or contextualizing) to individual neighborhood cultures. As Timothy Keller writes in *Center Church*:

"All gospel ministry and communication are already heavily adapted to a particular culture. So it is important to do contextualization *consciously*. If we never deliberately think through ways to rightly contextualize gospel ministry to a new culture, we will unconsciously be deeply contextualized to some other culture."[26]

To be fair, because neighborhoods in cities are constantly changing, this is probably a far more difficult task for long-established churches than church plants. My home church was a first-generation Korean American church planted in East Elmhurst, Queens, back when Korean immigrants were still living in the region or not too far from it. Today, it is a predominantly Hispanic neighborhood. To ask Koreans in East Elmhurst who neither speak Spanish nor understand the culture to contextualize to such an area might be asking for a bit too much.

But at the very least, churches are called to show that we care. One of the ways in which my previous church accomplished this was through inviting Hispanic residents of the neighborhood to have a separate service inside the church, free of rent. However, a potential danger to be wary about in such a method is that we could slip into the routine of doing something kind for the local people without the burden of actual interaction. As we will see later when discussing the value of generosity, the Bible calls us to all levels of sacrificial generosity, including the act of being *relationally* generous.

4. Being missional must be part of our church culture.

Over the years, churches have compartmentalized duties. We have evangelism teams, worship teams, mission teams, welcoming/greeting teams, prayer teams, setup teams, etc., and such teams are all good and necessary. But it should not take a title or a team for us to be missional in nature. For example, yes, the extroverts that are gifted in greeting (basically, the most outwardly pleasant people) should absolutely be at the front doors welcoming people in, but *everyone* in the congregation should be a welcomer/greeter. We should not need that specific title/role to approach a newcomer who is sitting by his/herself, or warmly say "hello" to the unfamiliar person standing next to us. Being missional is at the heart of what is means to be a Christian and what the church is called to do.[27]

About twelve years ago, I listened to a message by David Gibbons, lead pastor of Newsong Church in Santa Ana, California, where he challenged the listeners with this simple question, "Why can't we just love for the sake of loving? Why do we always need an agenda?"[28] It's a challenge that I've been humbled by since then, because so many of my acts of love have been motivated by my desire to be a good teacher, pastor, or church-goer, rather than a desire to love without personal agenda. It's what many of us do. We are driven to be good at our various church positions because it's what we've been told to do, or a desire to be seen as righteous by others. But what if those titles were stripped away from us? What if no one was keeping count or taking notes, not even ourselves? Would we still love, just because that's what the gospel moves us to do? It is with such a challenge that we must repeatedly and carefully examine the core of our motivations.

5. We must be missional both inside and outside the church.

Differences in the way we conduct ourselves *outside* the church or around non-believers also tell us something about the motivations behind our good behaviors, especially if such conduct is inconsistent with our behavior *inside* the church or around other believers.

I worked bi-vocationally as a pastor and as an attorney for five years. During that time, some of my most powerful ministry moments ironically took place outside of traditional "ministry" settings, such as a church or small group meeting. Just prior to opening my first law firm in New Jersey back in 2009, my former partner Aaron and I arrived at the office the night before, spread out our sleeping bags on the floor, got on our knees, and we prayed out loud with a sense of desperation. We prayed that we would display qualities of the Biblical fruit of the Spirit.

"But the fruit of the Spirit is love, joy, peace, forbearance, kindness, goodness, faithfulness, gentleness and self-control. Against such things there is no law." (Galatians 5:22-23)

And we sustained it for a bit. After one year, I split off from the partnership and ran my own solo practice in order to have more flexibility to focus on church ministry. As an attorney, I have stories of God moving powerfully in my practice in ways that I did not experience even as a pastor. I once felt led to pray for a struggling woman who had lost both her husband and father during the same year. She initially came to my office to probate her husband's will, but after the prayer, she broke down right in front of me. I later discovered from a pastor who called me a few days later to say "thank you" that the woman had returned to church after losing her faith. The prayer at my office reminded her that God had not given up on her. I realized that I did not need to be a pastor or inside the walls of a church building to be used by God, and that the Holy Spirit could work through me in my everyday life just as powerfully.

Unfortunately, if I'm being honest here, for every one of those stories, I have several that I am utterly ashamed of. As I continued living bi-vocationally, over time, I noticed a rather large discrepancy in the power of the gospel between my church and work life. Over the years, through examining my own heart, I thought of three possible reasons why Christians might separate our lives inside and outside the church walls:

The first, is the most straightforward; that separating our church and secular lives is simply what we've been taught, indoctrinated, or conditioned to do. But as I mentioned before, church is not a building we go to, it is our identity, it is who we are (Ephesians 1:22). And therefore, our identity should not change depending on our physical location.

The second possible explanation might sound a bit bizarre, but for some, church might serve as a sort of escape from reality, like an alternate life or alter ego, a trip away from the burdens of the real world. The rush of being Spiderman for one day of the week and the comfort of slipping back into Peter Parker for the other six (or vice versa, depending on how one wishes to view it). Or for others, there may be a feeling of comfort in minimal commitment to godly behavior; Sundays are to simply get one's soul fed by doing the "Christian stuff" we're supposed to do, and then walk out the doors and continue to live freely in whatever way we please. Both these scenarios use church as a tool to fill some sort of missing piece in one's life, but neither approach will result in transformation, and neither is true to God's call for us to live in Him authentically (1 John 1:5-7).

The third possible reason is the one I wish to discuss the most in depth. Perhaps some of us live these double lives because we believe what we do inside the church matters more than what we do outside, and I want to make the very bold statement that I strongly believe it's the other way around. Take this passage in Matthew for example:

"And when you pray, do not be like the hypocrites, for they love to pray standing in the synagogues and on the street corners to be seen by others. Truly I tell you, they have received their reward in full. But when you pray, go into your room, close the door and pray to your Father, who is unseen. Then your Father, who sees what is done in secret, will reward you." (Matthew 6:5-6)

This is a case where Jesus is using hyperbole to make a point. After all, he himself had obviously prayed outside of his room at some points in his ministry (we can always tell it's an overstatement if he's done the very thing he's instructing us not to do). The message Christ is making here is that it is the things we do when others aren't giving us credit for doing them that truly reveals our heart. Or, as William R. Moody says (paraphrasing his father, popular American evangelist D.L. Moody), "Character is what you are in the dark."[29]

To rephrase for the context of this discussion, a Christian's true character is revealed in the things they do outside of the church, such as being patient and exhibiting self-control towards that co-worker or classmate who annoys you, being kind and loving towards your family, being faithful in your walk with God in the privacy of your own room, etc.

Moody's statement, and the realization that my behavior was consistently inconsistent inside and outside the church walls, revealed flaws in my own character. I was a loving, kind, patient, and gentle person around congregation members (and I was regularly receiving praise for such attributes), but in my law firm I would frequently shout at and even kick out those who bothered me, turning into someone I never thought I was capable of becoming, a man who abused power. After a couple of years of practicing law, the prayers for me to be an attorney who displayed the fruit of the Spirit appeared to be a distant memory. It was too difficult for me to keep it up; I had given up on the cause. I was often ashamed to look at myself in the mirror, feeling like a hypocrite anytime I stepped into my office.

The problem was that I had forgotten that the fruit of the Spirit is meant to be just that, *fruit*, meaning it is the *result* of the Spirit's working in our lives. Attributes like patience, kindness, gentleness, and self-control are not themselves what we're supposed to be aiming for; instead, they are the natural byproducts of what we're truly supposed to be aiming for, which is encountering Jesus and allowing him to move in our hearts daily. Instead, I was trying to produce the fruit of the Spirit through my own efforts.

During that period of struggle, I woke up one morning with a deep sense of desperation, and I earnestly prayed to Jesus to show up in my life as I was warming up my car. I wanted to change, I wanted him to instruct me on what needed to be done. He did show up, but instead of telling me what to do, he showed me who I was in his eyes, that I was precious to him and worth dying for.

I was then reminded of the story of Jesus' baptism. The Spirit of God came down on him like a dove, and the voice of God told him, **"This is my Son, whom I love; with him I am well pleased"** (Matthew 3:17). For me, that image was so beautiful. It was the scene of a loving father looking down from the heavens at His son, His perfect son, and being totally, utterly, one hundred percent, *pleased.* And yet, when Christ went to the cross, it was the exact opposite. On the cross, Christ received the full wrath of God in our place, and we were clothed with Christ's righteousness. And now, instead of receiving the wrath of God (which we deserve), God looks at us the same way He once looked down from the heavens at His perfect child; He is totally, utterly, one hundred percent, *pleased.*

I cried that morning with my forehead pressed against the steering wheel as I felt so unworthy of His sacrificial love and grace, repeatedly hearing the words in my head, "David, you are my son, whom I love; with you I am well pleased."

Later that day, I received a phone call almost immediately after I walked into my office.

"Hello?" the frantic voice of a young woman spoke up on the other end of the line. "Please, I am in need of your help. I have no money, I'm desperate, and I need your help."

Right away I thought this was bad for business. Someone who needed my help and had no money was generally not positive news.

But instead of trying to exit the conversation like usual, I inquired for her to explain further.

She informed me that she was only nineteen years old and temporarily living out of her friend's house with her three-year-old son. She had gotten into a car accident not too long ago and fled the scene in a panic. The court then sent her a summons to appear tomorrow, and she was terrified because she needed her license and vehicle so that she could drive back and forth to work to provide for her son.

Once again, a part of me thought of escaping the conversation. Then something inside reminded me of the gospel, and I thought, *who am I not to show this woman grace?* I instructed her to meet me right outside the courtroom the next day, and I told her she wouldn't have to pay. She cried instantly upon hearing those words. She sobbed on that phone for quite some time, repeatedly telling me, "Thank you, thank you..."

The next day, I met her at the court and explained to the prosecutor her situation. Thankfully, because she had a clean record, he agreed to a plea-deal where she would simply pay a fine and retain her license and vehicle, and given her financial situation, the judge also granted my request to extend the fine for as long as statutorily allowed. Afterwards, we went back to the waiting room to get called in by the clerk for the final paperwork. Since attorneys typically saw the judge first, the room was still packed with about sixty people waiting to go inside.

Suddenly, standing there in the midst of that crowd, I felt compelled to ask if I could pray for her. She agreed while holding her little boy's hand, still grateful for what had just taken place. I prayed, but the room was so loud I could barely hear myself, and so I ended up shouting out my words, "LORD! PLEASE BE WITH THIS WOMAN! COMFORT HER!" Again, she cried as I prayed out loud. I must've looked like a complete lunatic to most of those people, but that's how I knew it wasn't from me; ordinarily, I would never have had the courage to do something like that. The gospel moved me to have compassion on that woman; she needed to hear my prayers. It wasn't about me, it was about *Christ*.

After I was done, she thanked me again and instantly opened up about her life. Her father was a pastor, but when she was just sixteen, she had a child out of wedlock and her father disowned her out of shame. Since then, she had been moving from friend's house to friend's house with her son, bitter towards her father, the church, and basically all Christians. She had lost her faith in God for the last three years, but meeting me reminded her of what she once had with the Lord. It gave her a sense of hope in her seemingly hopeless situation. After I gave her information about the church I was attending at the time, we embraced and parted ways, and I couldn't help but feel like I had done nothing, but Jesus had done everything. My compassion for this young woman didn't come from my own efforts or courage, it came from being with my Savior and allowing him to speak his words of love to me first.

Therefore, when it comes to being missional outside the church, we can go one of two ways. We can try to live as moral a life as we can on our own strength, hoping that will attract people to Christ. Unfortunately, because of our sinful natures, we will inevitably fail and become discouraged. (Even if we succeed, we'll grow arrogant like the Pharisees.) Not to mention, our failure will hurt our witness to the unchurched. Or, we can spend time with Jesus, seek him daily, and allow him to move in us so that we may display his fruit, and the world will know of his unfailing love through our sacrificial lives.

Spirit and Truth

I was inspired to add this value after reading Douglas Banister's *The Word and Power Church*, wherein he urges Christians to know God both intellectually and experientially.[30] Perhaps the most straightforward and concise Biblical passage on this matter is found in the book of John:

"God is spirit, and his worshipers must worship in the Spirit and in truth." (John 4:24)

The first part of the verse characterizes God as "spirit," with spirit in lowercase, meaning John is not speaking about the person of the Holy Spirit but rather, spirit as an attribute of God. John is saying that not only can God be experienced through the physical world (through nature and the like), He also transcends the physical world and connects with us through *feelings*, *emotions*, and *sensations*. The latter "Spirit" in the verse *is* referring to the Holy Spirit, the one who allows us to directly connect with God our father (Matthew 10:20) in a way that transcends the physical realm. Finally, the verse says that we not only worship God in the Spirit, but also in truth. Our relationship with God must be grounded in Scripture so that we are not easily led astray by our emotions (which are easily manipulated) or by bad theology and bad teaching.

Strangely, the subject of *intellectual* vs. *experiential* Christianity has become a polarizing issue in the church today, when in fact, these concepts are in no way mutually exclusive. Furthermore, Bannister makes the argument that many Christians are tired of the "either-or" mentality of the church.[31]

To be fair, there are historical reasons for this current controversy. In the past, a strong movement of charismatics (otherwise known today as the more "spiritual" Christians) began emphasizing the importance of a more experiential spirituality, while at the same time downplaying a more intellectual engagement with God and the Scriptures, which they regarded as incompatible with the idea of a personal, relational God. Unfortunately, such a view could at times result in the harmful emotional manipulation of Christians. For instance, Bannister recalls once seeing a sign outside a Pentecostal church in his town which read, "No tongues, no salvation". Even Jack Deere, the well-known charismatic pastor and theologian, acknowledges abuse by certain charismatic movements in *Surprised by the Power of Spirit*:

"It is undeniable that there are significant abuses within some groups that believe in and practice the gifts of the Spirit. I have witnessed emotionalism, exaggerations, elitism, prophetic words used in a controlling and manipulative way, and a lack of spiritual foundation in various meetings and movements. I would not say, however, that this is true of the majority of the groups..."[32]

Historically, when charismatics went to such extremes, Christians who espoused a more intellectual approach to faith reacted with their own form of extremism that discounted *all* forms of experiential Christianity. Even today, I have Christian friends who scoff whenever I utter the words *Holy Spirit* (which, by the way, is mentioned roughly ninety times in the New Testament).

Sadly, we tend to classify other churches and other Christians as belonging to one of these two extremes, instead of exploring and incorporating the best aspects of both traditions so that we can experience the full breadth and power of the gospel in our lives. The danger in completely discounting experiential Christianity is that it is impossible to have a deep and personal relationship with God without at least some level of connection involving feelings or emotions. The Bible describes God as our *father* (Matthew 6:26), our *spouse* (Isaiah 54:5), and our *friend* (James 2:23), all forms of deep relationships that involve strong feelings and emotions, and not merely a connection based on intellectual knowledge. Surely the Bible would not use such terms to describe our relationship with God if we were only meant to connect with Him intellectually.

To illustrate, when my parents got divorced when I was six, there was no doubt in my mind that my father still loved me. After all, he was my dad, and I had always been told that dads were supposed to love their children. But knowing that he loved me and experiencing his love were two different things.

One of my clearest memories from childhood is waiting for my dad to come pick up my brother and I on the weekends. I would stare out the window anticipating for his arrival and as soon as I saw his car coming down the street, I would dash down the stairs as fast I could. I'd fling open the door and sprint into his arms, and he would pick me up, squeeze me tight, swirl me around, and kiss me on the top of my head and all over my face while repeatedly telling me, "I love you! I love you! I love you!" (Unlike the typical immigrant parent, my father was very affectionate towards my brother and I, especially when we were younger.) Although I already knew intellectually that my father loved me, and that knowledge gave me a certain level of comfort, it was the *experience* of being loved by him in person that deepened the relationship and brought it to life. And so it is with God.

However, I feel compelled to mention that churches need to be extremely careful in defining what an *experience* with God actually requires. There are some who enter a church with high production values (bright lights, multimedia presentations, a talented worship team, etc.) and say, "Wow, the Spirit is *really* here!" While there are ninety references to the Holy Spirit in the New Testament, at no point does the Bible ever mention the Spirit being more present when the production level of a church is higher or more grandiose.

Don't get me wrong; it's very possible that the Spirit is moving powerfully in a church with high production values, and I have no objection to bright lights and talented worship teams. The question for us to reflect on is, what are we using such things for? If it's truly to glorify God, great. Heaven acknowledges and honors various forms of expression in our worship (Revelation 14:2). But we must be clear that these things are not themselves a prerequisite for experiencing the presence of the Holy Spirit. When the Holy Spirit came upon the apostles at Pentecost, it wasn't because of the sophisticated presentation of the gospel at their gathering. In the same way, no church can simply throw money, talent, and efforts together in an effort to conjure the presence and power of the Holy Spirit.

I once visited the house of a good pastoral buddy of mine. After a while, we went into one of his rooms to pray. No music, no singing, no production. We just sat there in silence and *listened*. In the quiet, I was able to reflect with God in a manner that felt genuinely free of distraction, and He revealed to me several things I needed to see about the condition of my heart. I am not saying every encounter with God must be this way, and again, I am not speaking against grandiose church productions as a means of facilitating spiritual connection, but the Biblical truth is that the Spirit cannot be conjured by man. The Spirit is *always* here with believers (John 14:16). It does not, and should not, take fancy man-made productions in order for us to have an experience with God, and this truth should be made clear to congregations that depend on the Sunday bright lights for an encounter with Him. We should be encouraging our members to also seek Him in the ordinary, quieter moments of our lives (1 Thessalonians 5:17).

In addition to connecting with God through the Spirit, the Bible also calls us to walk with Him **"...in truth"** (John 4:24). However, Christians who take a more intellectual approach to their faith must also acknowledge that connecting with God on an intellectual level still requires discernment through the Spirit so that we don't mistake our own "wisdom" for God's.

Not to get too philosophical here (because we can then go on forever into an abyss), but what is truth anyway, and who gets to decide? Does everyone get to define truth for themselves? Is it merely whatever we want to believe or feel? If that's the case, there is no such thing as objective truth.

For example, I'm a diehard New York Mets fan (I know, it's been a long and difficult journey). Suppose that in the Fall of 2015, when the Mets went to the World Series, I was locked in a room for a year and never told the outcome of the Series. And suppose that during my time in the locked room, I was able to convince myself that the Mets actually won the World Series, so much so that when I was released into the real world a year later, no one could convince me that the Royals actually won in five games. As far as I was concerned, the "truth" was that the Mets had won the series.

The above illustrates the danger when truth simply becomes whatever we feel or desire to believe. In our postmodern world, there is a growing sentiment, even among the religious, that God himself is whoever we want Him to be. The problem with such a belief is that God is then not God at all; He is merely an extension of your own personality and beliefs. Therefore, you are actually making *yourself* God.

A year ago, I was at a bookstore looking through the Christian book section when a man who appeared to be in his mid-thirties approached me and asked if I believed in Jesus Christ.

"Yes," I replied.

"Right on, brother!" he cheered, as he enthusiastically applauded my answer. "I believe in him too, dude!" Naturally, I assumed he must be a Christian. He paused momentarily to scratch his head and then continued, "The only thing is, I don't think he was the son of God or anything like that, but he was a great dude, that's for sure. He influenced our society in many positive ways, teaching us things like turning the other cheek and loving one another. That dude was awesome, bro!"

Normally, in such a random setting with a total stranger, I wouldn't have engaged very deeply in such a conversation. But I felt this statement was just too nonsensical to ignore.

I responded, "The issue I have with that belief is that Jesus *claimed* he was the son of God. Historically, that's what's been documented, and that's the message that the first century Christians spread. He *said* specifically that he was the son of God. Furthermore, during his time in ministry, he managed to convince many who were close to him that he was, in fact, the son of God. Now if he was not the son of God, then he couldn't have possibly been a 'great' and 'awesome' dude. He would have to be the world's biggest liar, phony, and hoax. So, it's either you believe he was the son of God, or the only alternative is that you believe he was an abject liar who conned many into believing a terrible lie."

The man thought about it for a (very brief) moment, and then replied while shrugging his shoulders nonchalantly, "I just wanna believe this version of Jesus, alright man? I'll just believe my version and you believe yours. What's so wrong with that?"

I realized from the conversation that in postmodern thought, we rarely question the ridiculousness of believing whatever we want to believe, simply because that's what currently *feels right*. But history shows that what feels right at a societal level is constantly changing. There are many things that felt right two hundred years ago that no longer feel right today. Take for example, slavery, racism, and sexism. Likewise, we don't know what are the things that are acceptable today that will be considered unacceptable in society two hundred years from now. How then can we trust ourselves to know what is the truth about what is good and right?

The truth also changes at an individual level as we age. When I was ten, it felt right to watch television all day (and I would've if my mom didn't stop me). Then when I was twenty, it felt right to watch television all day as long as I had my studies/work done. When I was in my late twenties, it felt right to watch television but only in moderation even if I had nothing else to do. And now in my mid-thirties, outside of one or two shows, I view television as a complete waste of my time. If my personal truth on the proper amount of television to consume is constantly changing as I age, how can I trust myself to know the truth about anything?

Because individuals and societies as a whole are constantly changing and evolving, we cannot be trusted to discern the truth about God on our own. We need something to guide us, and that's where Scripture comes in. God the father has always been the same, and therefore, Christ and the message of the gospel has always been the same (Hebrews 13:8). He does not change along with the times or with age. God remains constant in His desires and nature.

The Bible gives us an unchanging truth that we can use to check our own beliefs and feelings. For years, church leaders have made questionable decisions based solely off their own feelings, and without considering whether such decisions might actually contradict God's desires (or they were aware and simply chose to ignore these contradictions for their own selfish gains). A good example of this is the corruption of the Roman Catholic Church during the sixteenth century when church leaders sold indulgences with the stated purpose of absolving people of their sins. When reading Scripture, it is plain to see that the practice of selling indulgences contradicts the promise from Christ Jesus that salvation comes simply through faith and faith alone (Galatians 3:10-14).

In response to such contradictions, Martin Luther, the founder of the Protestant Reformation spoke these words at the Diet of Worms (when asked to recant the Ninety-five Theses that was nailed to the castle door at Wittenberg):

"*Unless I am convicted by Scripture* (emphasis added) and plain reason–I do not accept the authority of the popes and councils, for they have contradicted each other–my conscience is captive to the Word of God. I cannot and I will not recant anything for to go against conscience is neither right nor safe."[33]

A common worldly refrain is that one should "follow your heart." But the truth is, our hearts are too changeable and our feelings can't be trusted (even if we have good intentions and believe we are working for the good of God's kingdom). Instead, we must let Scripture have full authority over our hearts and feelings and become "captive to the Word of God."[34] Consider these words from Kee Won Huh, a pastor at New Mercy Community Church in Edgewater, New Jersey:

"There is a difference between conviction and truth. Too many Christians feel if they are convicted about something, that conviction somehow automatically lends weight and legitimacy to their belief or position. And, often, they leverage this supposed weight to persuade others.

71

Unfortunately, what we often fail to realize is that we can be convicted about something that is completely false. Sheer convictional fiat should never persuade anyone. People are convicted that salt rocks exude a health-giving aura, but they're very much wrong about that conviction. A Christian man may feel convicted that a particular girl is destined to be his wife (even saying that God told him so); but often, over time, these men end up feeling convicted in this way regarding multiple women. Other Christians feel convicted they can predict the end of the world despite the fact Jesus clearly teaches otherwise. Even Hitler was convicted about his beliefs, but he was dead wrong. Christians must test their convictions with the Word, with general revelation, in prayer, and with honest community that can speak counter to your beliefs when you are wrong (a body over you, not a body you lead). It is often the case that conviction without accountability leads to attitudes and actions that are completely counter to the will of God. Be careful about those who try to "argue" you to their position because of their conviction. Passion is not the measure of truth. Truth is truth regardless of the emotions and convictions attached to it. One can feel completely indifferent about God, yet that does not diminish His reality in the least."[35]

To put this into practice, suppose I feel convicted that God is calling me to abandon my wife and two kids to become a missionary overseas in a foreign country. Even though I may in that moment feel rock-solid conviction this is the right thing to do, if I were to check in with the Word, Scripture would tell me that Biblically, I am called to be united and one with my wife (Genesis 2:24), love and sacrifice for her the way Christ did for me (Ephesians 5:25), and that I am to honor my marriage (Hebrews 13:4). Furthermore, I would be blatantly dismissing my Biblical responsibility to instruct and discipline my children (Ephesians 6:4) and to influence them in a positive manner (Proverbs 22:6).

Even if we concede that Scripture is the ultimate authority over our lives, we would then still have to be wary about the manner in which we apply its teachings. *Context is absolutely key.* Biblical passages need to be studied in accordance with its historical context (the political, social, and cultural circumstances during which the text was written).[36] Therefore, it is helpful to have a reliable study guide or commentary nearby when reading the Word. If we claim Scripture is essential, but we solely use our own uninformed feelings or judgment to interpret its meaning, we're right back to becoming our own discerners about who God is.

For example, some years back, I was walking through the cafeteria of my former church where some congregation members were selling food and lemonade to raise money in order to help cancer patients. I overheard a group of disgruntled women standing nearby complaining that this practice was against the Biblical passage in Matthew 21:12-13 where Jesus drove out those who were selling goods in the temple courts.

Now if one read the passage from Matthew with absolutely no knowledge of its context, it is possible to interpret it to mean that we should never sell anything in the house of God for any reason. But when examining what's actually going on in the story, we realize it was not the selling of goods that upset Jesus, but rather that the sellers were taking advantage of the poor through inflating prices of animals that were deemed worthy of sacrifice during the Passover Feast. Thus, rather than interpreting the passage as one against selling goods in church, it should be understood as a warning against cheating the poor and taking advantage of the vulnerable and disenfranchised. Without a proper understanding of the historical and cultural context that this story takes place in, we run the risk of grossly misrepresenting Jesus' character. After all, during his ministry Jesus was clearly *for* helping the sick over enforcing moralistic rules (Mark 3:1-6).

As a child, I used to go to various Christian programs where they would teach me to close my eyes, open the Bible, point anywhere inside, open my eyes, read the verse, and say what God was telling me in that moment through those words, as if reading the Bible was a magic trick. But it is not a magic trick; it is the *truth*, and we cannot rely on our own subjective analysis to determine the truth.

Moreover, instead of letting the Scriptures be the basis upon which we form our principles and beliefs, we have a tendency to cherry-pick passages in the Bible that validate beliefs we already possess. An example of this is the traditional church practice of viewing tattoos as a sin. Often times, such beliefs are reinforced with passages such as 1 Corinthians 6:19 **("Do you not know that your bodies are temples of the Holy Spirit, who is in you, whom you have received from God?")** or Leviticus 19:28 **("Do not cut your bodies for the dead or put tattoo marks on yourselves")**. To be clear, I am not suggesting everyone rush to get tattoos without questioning their own personal motives for doing so (Proverbs 16:18) or without examining if such things could possibly be a hindrance to other nonbelievers, depending on one's context, of course (1 Corinthians 10:23, 31-33). But it should be noted that these passages do not give blanket rulings on the matter of tattoos: in fact, they do not address the matter at all. They are speaking on sexual immorality (1 Corinthians 6:18-20) and the pagan customs of intentionally creating religious pagan patterns on one's body (Leviticus 19:28).

Traditionalists would argue that the words in the passages provide an overarching principle that can similarly be applied to tattoos. But the problem then becomes knowing how far to stretch that principle. Where do we draw the line? If Scripture contradicts a traditionally held belief, are we willing to move the line or will we stubbornly hold on to man-made traditions rather than letting the Word transform those traditions to be more in line with the truthful desires of God?

Perhaps the most egregious example of holding on to man-made traditions despite Scriptures to the contrary is the practice of slavery. Proponents of slavery frequently pointed to passages such as Ephesians 6:5 **("Slaves, obey your earthly masters with respect and fear, and with sincerity of heart, just as you would obey Christ")** as evidence that slavery was an institution ordained by God. But when examining the passage in Ephesians in its entirety, it becomes clear that the Apostle Paul is not condoning slavery, but rather, he is instructing people on how to continue to live Biblically within the boundaries of their current situations (Ephesians 6:1-9). Also, historically the slaves in the New Testament context were more akin to indentured servants rather than the form of slavery with Africans that was practiced in the United States. There is absolutely no way one can study and understand the New Testament within its proper context,

74

especially the ministry of Jesus himself, and not recognize that the heart of Christ was to raise the status of the oppressed. When "Christians" ignored the historical and cultural context of the Scriptures to justify slavery, they were creating their own morality to serve their own purposes instead of submitting to the Word.

Thus, to circle back to our original point, in order to truly understand the will of God, His character, and His desires, it is essential to seek to encounter God both experientially and intellectually. Although we know studying Scripture is essential to understanding the will of God, His character, and His desires, it is still not a substitute for loving Him, and vice versa. John Piper, the well-known Calvinist Baptist preacher and an advocate of the relatively new intellectual-based reformed movement, was asked in an interview, "John, would there be any cautions you would have for this new reformed, Calvinist movement?"[37] His answer:

"My caution concerns making theology God instead of God, God. Loving doing theology rather than loving God. And you might love thinking about God more than you love God. Or defending God more than you love God. Or writing about God more than you love God. Or preaching more than you love God. Or evangelizing more than you love God. The kind of person that is prone to systematize and fit things together, like me, is wired dangerously to begin to idolize the system. We should be intellectually and emotionally more engaged with the person of Christ, the person of God, the Trinity, than we are with thinking about Him. Thinking about God and engaging with Him are inextricably woven together. But the reason you are reading the Bible, and the reason you are framing thoughts about God from the Bible, is to make your way through those thoughts to the real person."[38]

Piper's point in a nutshell is that the entire purpose of studying theology is so that we may develop a deep and personal relationship with our Father. In the absence of this relationship, we've merely made theology itself our "God."

Bannister in *The Word and Power Church* references the Pietists, a group that formed in the seventeenth century, and who were strongly rooted in the Word, but at the same time coined the popular phrase "a personal relationship with Jesus", which we still use to this day.[39] While most Christians in those days sang songs *about* Jesus, the Pietists sang songs *to* Jesus, for they believed it wasn't enough to just know him, but that they needed to fall in love with him.[40]

We can study the Word inside out, know of God's character, even understand His desires, but unless He is the father that squeezes us tightly, picks us up, swirls us around, and kisses us all over our faces and on the top of our heads while repeatedly telling us, "I love you! I love you! I love you," He is not truly the God of the cross in our life. For the gospel tells us He sacrificed His only son so that we can now not just know *of* His love, but also to *experience* it as well.

Diversity

In the summer of 1996, when I was only fourteen years old, I, along with a **Y**outh **W**ith **A** **M**ission ("YWAM")[41] team from Richmond, Virginia, attended *Target World* in Atlanta, Georgia. The purpose of this collaborative YWAM event was to gather together thousands of Christians from various countries for worship under the same roof for a period of one week. As a young teenager, to witness such an event was absolutely breathtaking; no one had to teach me that thousands of people from different ethnicities, tongues, cultures, and backgrounds worshipping together was a beautiful sight. I simply knew from the chills in my body. It reminded me of the church the Bible describes in a passage from Revelation:

"After this I looked, and there before me was a great multitude that no one could count, from every nation, tribe, people, and language, standing before the throne and before the Lamb." (Revelation 7:9)

But what if I made the argument that diversity is not only positive, but *necessary,* for building God's kingdom?

What is diversity in the church, from a Biblical perspective? In the book of Galatians, the Apostle Paul describes a few sources of division that may arise in the body of Christ:

77

"In Christ, there is neither Jew nor Greek, there is neither slave nor free, there is neither male nor female; for you are all one in Christ Jesus." (Galatians 3:28)

We notice in the passage the potential divisions of *race/culture* (**"Jew nor Greek"**), *socioeconomic status* (**"slave nor free"**), and *gender* (**"male nor female"**). (Given Paul's specific cultural and historical context, to imply that women and men were equal was particularly bold and revolutionary.) In 1 Timothy 4:12, Paul addresses yet another possible source of division: *age*. Despite these divisions, Paul proclaims that we are all one in Christ Jesus and he lays out the foundation for church diversity: people of different races, cultures, socioeconomic backgrounds, genders, and/or age groups coming together as a family because our common identity in Christ trumps our differences.

In our current cultural context, when we speak about diversity, most people automatically think about racial diversity. However, fixating on one type of diversity can sometimes lead to an impractical bind. For example, if I'm speaking to my buddy who's planting a church in Washington Heights, New York, a predominantly Dominican neighborhood, the fact of the matter is that there is only so racially diverse that the church is going to be given the demographics of the neighborhood. Certainly, no church planter possesses the power to make his neighborhood more racially/culturally diverse. (Even if that was possible, the impact that churches can have on the racial and cultural demographics of a neighborhood is a tricky ethical grey area, particularly if an area is being stripped of its historical cultural identity.) Similarly, when I talk to a first-generation Korean pastor whose congregation mainly speaks only Korean, how do I encourage them to be racially diverse?

Plain answer, I can't. Forced diversity is impractical and almost certain to end in disaster. That being said, there are always ways to work on diversity. Because no matter how homogenous a community looks from the outside, there will always be forces acting to pull that community apart. Perhaps for the church in Washington Heights, encouraging diversity means bringing different age groups together to bridge the gap between the generations. And maybe in the first-generation Korean church where culturally, societal status is frequently emphasized as the basis of one's identity, the challenge would be to encourage people to cast aside differences in social standing and to love and accept one another as brothers and sisters in the family of Jesus Christ (1 Corinthians 12:22-25). When a church in Washington Heights brings three generations worshipping together under the same roof and a first-generation Korean church treats all of its members as equals in the body, surely such unusual behavior will catch the attention of those who are familiar with the typical divisions in such contexts.

Still, the fact remains that bringing diverse groups of people together has its challenges, which is why it is much more common to see churches of a single race/ethnicity, socioeconomic class, and age group as its general congregational makeup. Rich Villodas, who's currently the lead pastor of New Life Fellowship in Elmhurst, Queens, an extremely diverse church in almost every sense, describes this struggle as follows: "Those who romanticize the diverse church have 1) never led one or 2) subscribes to a superficial diversity strategy...This is hard work!"[42]

In fact, Biblically, diversity was not a cake-walk either for the first century church, even in a place like Antioch where Christian Jewish missionaries were sent for the sole purpose of ministering to the Gentiles (non-Jews). You would think that with such a clear mission, these missionaries would be able to put aside their differences for the greater cause. After all, many of these missionaries, including the Apostle Paul, were willing to risk their lives for the gospel. Unfortunately, the attitude of many Jewish Christians was still defined by their man-made traditions rather than by the gospel.

A popular example of when diversity in the first century church failed is found in a passage from Galatians where the Apostle Paul confronted Peter for separating himself from the Gentiles when the traditional Jewish group arrived, saying:

"When Cephas (Peter) came to Antioch, I opposed him to his face, because he stood condemned. For before certain men came from James, he used to eat with the Gentiles. But when

they arrived, he began to draw back and separate himself from the Gentiles because he was afraid of those who belonged to the circumcision group." (Galatians 2:11-12)

Peter and the traditional Jewish group failed to realize that cultivating diversity also includes embracing the various ways in which different cultures and traditions celebrate the gospel. There is no *one* way to worship God and we should not judge those who worship in a way that differs from our own (Romans 14:3).

For example, while many people express themselves through fashion and what they wear, my clothing has nothing to do with my self-expression. Most of my t-shirts are related to Star Wars or the Mets and I've worn the same pair of blue jeans for years. That's just the way I am. I do dress decently for Sunday service, but that's mostly because my wife chooses my outfits on Sundays. For me, giving God my Sunday best means prayerfully preparing my heart prior to going to church; presenting a well-dressed outer appearance has nothing to do with it. Nevertheless, even though I do not relate to this particular form of expressing my worship to God, I must acknowledge that when people do give God their best through dressing up (because it's a part of their personal context, culture, or tradition), it's a beautiful thing and I must not judge but rather affirm them. It is essential for the sake of diversity that we keep an open mind about such things.

However, I must pause here for a huge disclaimer that needs to be emphasized. Although the gospel is meant to be celebrated through different traditions, we have to be careful not to make the tradition itself the gospel. In my early-twenties, I had a close atheist friend who had a mother that was suffering from cancer. I'll never forget when my friend called me on the phone one night while crying and trembling in anger. When I asked her what was wrong, she explained that her mother had started to attend church once again to renew her faith during her final years, but when she walked into the sanctuary of a well-known megachurch in Queens, a woman immediately approached her and asked her to remove her hat. However, her mother was extremely self-conscious because she was losing her hair due to the chemotherapy, and so she kindly asked the woman if she could keep it on due to her condition. But the woman obstinately presented the ultimatum that if she did not remove her hat, she would have to leave the service. And so she took off the hat and cried in shame for the remainder of her time there. The heartbreaking words of my friend that night still resonate with me till this day, "David, I know all about Jesus, and I've read all about him too, he seems wonderful and I so badly want to be a Christian, but you people make it *so easy* for me to hate you." I could not dispute her words, because I knew them to be true. When a church allows someone to be shamed or excluded for the sake of keeping their traditions, they are not about the gospel–they are about their traditions.

This is best addressed in the book of Romans where certain Jewish Christians strongly emphasized the tradition of not eating meat:

"Accept the one whose faith is weak, without quarreling over disputable matters. One person's faith allows them to eat anything, but another, whose faith is weak, eats only vegetables." (Romans 14:1-2)

The real irony when reading the text is that often times when we use the term "weak" within the church context, we're referring to non-Christians or baby-Christians, generally people who haven't been exposed much to church. But the passage above specifically labels the weak as the ones who do not eat meat for the sake of placing their tradition over the gospel (the legalistic); they're the ones who mostly grew up in religious settings. In other words, it is entirely possible to be a lifetime church-goer, know the ins and outs of church culture, and yet still allow your tradition to be your gospel after all those years, or in Biblical terms, to be the *weak*.

Nevertheless, the gospel calls us to accept those who are difficult, stubborn, and wrongfully indoctrinated, for without acceptance, there can be no diversity. However, we learn from the previous passage where the Apostle Peter separated himself from the Gentiles that acceptance takes effort; that even Peter of all people, who went to Antioch for the primary purpose and mission of ministering to the Gentiles, fell back into separating himself from Gentiles (Galatians 2:11-12). The passage reminds us that while diversity is a good thing that all Christians should value, it can be uncomfortable, unnatural, and often takes intentionality.

I recently discussed the topic of diversity with a good pastoral buddy of mine. Despite the fact that we had both planted churches with racial diversity in mind, we both started out with core groups of mostly Asian Americans. To be fair, our church in Bayside, Queens is still far from the racially/culturally diverse congregation that I've been earnestly seeking and praying for. However, our church had been making progress at a rate faster than my friend's, which was ironically located in a far more racially/culturally diverse neighborhood. And so I asked him, "Why is it such a struggle for you guys? Considering your neighborhood and context, I'm sure you have people of different races and ethnicities visiting here and there."

To which he replied, "Do the Asian Americans in your core group really care about racial diversity?"

"Yes." The answer was a no brainer, mostly because many of them had negative experiences at their previous, predominantly Asian churches, and were seeking something different.

"See? That's the difference. Our Asians are very comfortable being around only other Asians. They won't really bother taking the extra step in reaching out to non-Asians when they visit our church."

If a congregation is not being *intentional* about encouraging diversity, then it is foolish to believe that it will just take place. While Christians often profess that they want to attend a diverse church, many do not want to step out of their comfort zones to make it a reality. As Bryan Loritts, lead pastor of Abundant Life Christian Fellowship in Mountain View, California, once said, "Your congregation will be as diverse as those who you invite to your dinner table."[43]

The reason achieving diversity is so difficult is because it not only challenges us in terms of our differences, but also in terms of our own innate desire to know and be known, to belong, and to continue after what we know.[44] For example, churches strive to be a "family," and yet this desire can become a brutally divisive force that results in rejecting newcomers because of the feeling of exclusivity that the idea of "family" naturally entails.[45] Furthermore, we can talk about intentionally trying to be a diverse church, but would it be authentic to the spirit of inclusion if the intent doesn't come from our hearts? Or are we only going through the motions for how we think a church that values diversity should operate?

In order to truly break the patterns of exclusivity we must first be secure in our own acceptance and identity as children of God through Christ's sacrifice. Only then will we be ready, willing, and expecting to make sacrifices for this cause. Only then will our intentionality for diversity and inclusion come from our hearts.

We know the gospel leads us to diversity, but here are some practical reasons why diversity is necessary.

1. The more homogenous we are, the more we are unable to understand the gospel in its entirety.

I previously mentioned the story of my friend John who had overheard a conversation between his two daughters, and how through the story I learned something from a child that I wouldn't have been able to gain from an adult. Because the way we relate to the gospel differs based on our individual experiences and stage of life, our understanding of the gospel is incomplete and fragmented. Therefore, if we're constantly surrounded by people who are just like us, we're only being exposed to one angle and one perspective of the good news.

To further elaborate, I have a buddy who by our society's standards did pretty well for himself in life: steady job, makes decent money, bought a nice house, found a lovely wife, etc. Let's just call him Rob. When I asked Rob about his faith in God, he explained it to me like this: "I don't know, it's like, God has always been looking out for me all my life. When I was a teenager, I did a lot of bad things, I dropped out of high school, I nearly dropped out of college too, but things always seemed to kind of fall into place. I met the right woman, the right people, the right opportunities opened up, and now here I am, so much to be thankful for. Through all of this, that's how I realized God was in full control of my life all along. I have faith in Him because He always had faith in me."

Now everything Rob said is theologically true; God was indeed in full control (Psalms 29:3-10). And there's something to be learned through his story about the sovereignty of God, that He is the ultimate

83

planner over our lives and we ought to trust in Him completely (Proverbs 3:5).

However, the lesson that God is in full control over our lives, although theologically true, is easier for a wealthy person to relate to as opposed to someone with less. A few years back, I went with several friends to Manhattan with food, water, and Bibles to minister to homeless people on the streets. I recall having a conversation with a homeless man under a bridge about his faith. I was astonished that he still held onto his beliefs despite his many years of hardships. "All this time man, I never once gave up my faith," he told me, with a large jovial grin, "I know the big man upstairs got somethin' real special waitin' for me in the kingdom of heaven even though I ain't got nothin' right now. And that's why I keep on prayin' to Him every night, 'cause He gives me hope."

Once again, everything this man spoke of was also theologically true, that God is our hope, where we find our rest, comfort, and security (Psalms 62:5), and the glorious inheritance for those who believe in Jesus Christ awaits us in the kingdom of heaven (Matthew 25:34). This poor man managed to live a gospel-centered life through focusing mostly on the hope promised for his future because of Christ's sacrifice.

Through Rob's story, I learned about *God's sovereignty*, and through the homeless man's story, I learned about *hope.* These two different men, speaking from completely different socioeconomic backgrounds, were able to illustrate to me two different but equally important aspects of the gospel. Through both their stories, I was able to gain a larger and more complete picture of what Jesus Christ meant for my own life.

2. Diversity is a powerful tool for evangelism.

When I began working as a solo-practitioner in New Jersey, I found that my inability to speak Korean proficiently was both an advantage and disadvantage as a Korean-American lawyer. I was at a disadvantage because I could not communicate well with potential Korean-speaking clients. (First and second-generation Koreans in New York and New Jersey existed in a very tightly knit community, and thus, I was missing out on an established system of referrals.) However, my inability to speak Korean was also an advantage because that forced me to branch out and expand my law practice into the non-Korean-speaking market. For several years, I was the only Korean-American solo-practitioner in all of Bergen County who was regularly going to court with almost all non-Korean clients.

Although I didn't want to attract attention to myself (because older attorneys frequently felt threatened by younger lawyers), it couldn't be helped since I stood out so much. It wasn't even that I was getting so many clients or making so much money (just ask my wife), it was that I was doing something rare and unique.

Over time, I had many people approach me at court; other attorneys, court interpreters, public defenders, prosecutors, even judges, and they'd all wonder how I was doing this. And the only answer I really had was that I was simply marketing/advertising to non-Koreans. To be honest, I didn't grow up around many Koreans, and so reaching non-Korean clients was not a very difficult task for me. And yet, something so simple blew the minds of many because, again, it was *unique*.

Similarly, when certain people heard I was planting a church in Bayside, Queens, they assumed it would be a second-generation Korean American church. Initially, that confused the heck out of me, and I wondered, why would anyone think that I would only minister to one age group and race/culture? And I realized, it's because they assumed I would take the road they perceived to be more convenient or familiar for me. This is probably something that some church leaders don't want to hear, but is there actually another legitimate reason for having an English-speaking church of exclusively one race/culture other than for convenience? That would be like the first century Jewish Christians going into an area like Antioch that has Gentiles and ministering to only Jews while separating themselves from the Gentiles, and we've already discussed why Peter was Biblically wrong for doing so (Galatians 2:11-12). Again, I am not talking about forcing diversity, but rather cultivating a spirit of inclusion.

As Christians, we are not called to do what's convenient or familiar. We're called to allow the gospel to move us out of our comfort zones and familiarity, and in turn love those who are different from ourselves so that the uniqueness and quality of our community will intrigue those looking in from the outside.

Last year, I sat down for a meal with a young atheist man in his mid-twenties who, until recently, had consistently attended church. When I asked him why he had stopped, he listed several reasons, but he capped it off by saying, "And you Christians can't even get along with each other; you have different churches for different race groups, you can't even make it work amongst yourselves and you expect people to want to join you?"

What I took away from the conversation was that not only does diversity help the Christian movement, but lack of diversity actually *hurts* it. Seen this way, diversity is not only an important value for a gospel-oriented church, it is an important tool for reaching and evangelizing to non-Christians and expanding God's kingdom. In short, diversity goes hand in hand with effective evangelism.

So I'll finish with this last question: how do people who are so different, who come from various backgrounds and stages of life, come together in acceptance of one another like they did in the first century church?

I'll answer with a story. On that very same YWAM trip I went on back when I was fourteen years old, once *Target World* was finished, our team drove out to a mountainous region for a group hike. During the hike, I was in the back with the one kid I could not stand, Jay. And lo and behold, he and I got into this huge argument, and we ended up staying behind to conclude our intense shouting match. Once we were finished, we noticed that the group had already moved on ahead out of our sights.

Like a couple of morons, we thought it would be a brilliant idea to cut across through the woods to meet them on the other side. So we started to trek through the woods, and after a while, we noticed we weren't reaching any trails or roads of any sort, but we had gone in way too deep to turn back. So we just kept on moving forward, and before we knew it, five hours had already gone by and we were completely lost. We had bumps and bruises everywhere, I got stung in the right leg by three bees simultaneously (couldn't make this stuff up)

86

and I had to physically lean on Jay for support during the latter part of our adventure. It was like a scene out of the popular 1986 film *Stand by Me*.[46]

During the fifth hour of wandering, we finally came upon a road and both of us collapsed on the side from exhaustion, lifelessly lying there waiting for someone to come to our rescue. During the eighth hour, it started to get dark, and the very real possibility that we were going to have to spend the night on the side of that road began to creep into our young horrified minds.

Then all of sudden, we noticed a bright pair of headlights approaching our way, and Jay and I quickly popped up to our feet and began to wave our eager arms in desperation. The car stopped next to us, and when we told them what happened, the lovely couple inside invited us to hop into the backseat where there were sandwiches and water for us to consume. We embraced tightly before we entered, ecstatically screaming out loud while bouncing up and down, "We're saved! We're saved!" Total joy had entered our once exhausted bodies. When the car took us back to our team, we ran out, for we couldn't wait to share our story with everyone else.

For the remainder of that trip, Jay and I became friends because our common experience enabled us to forge a bond despite our differences. The gospel tells us that regardless of race, gender, socioeconomic status, or age, we all share the same powerful story, that we were once left for dead on the side of that road, but the bright lights of Jesus Christ came to pick us up. We don't experience the gospel alone; we weren't meant to. We experience it together as a community, and thus, our magnificent story is something we can't wait to spread to others, no matter how different they are from us.

Generosity

In my early-twenties, a good childhood buddy of mine had a daughter at a relatively young age (for city standards). Although I was busy with my studies and preoccupied with going out with the early-twenties-singles city crowd, I made an effort to visit him and his wife a couple of times during their first year of parenthood and brought gifts for their newborn. For years, I just assumed he was doing okay, that he had moved on to a different chapter of his life, a chapter that didn't need me around as much.

Twelve years later, he unexpectedly confronted me saying, "David, why weren't you there for me when I first had my daughter?"

The conversation totally caught me off guard, because I genuinely thought I *was* there for him. "What are you talking about?" I responded, in a confused tone. "I visited you with gifts, remember?"

He shook his head in disappointment. "And what was that, like twice? I was a young man, bro, practically still a kid. I was scared, and I needed friends to be there for me. But you were too busy living your own life, doing your own thing. Let's be honest here, you didn't really care about me or my family."

I left that conversation feeling deeply apologetic and with so much to reflect on. I couldn't believe it. All those years I thought I was a generous friend because I had visited him a couple of times with gifts, but I failed to give him the one gift he actually needed, the gift of my time and friendship.

In the parable of the *Good Samaritan*, a man is beaten, robbed, and left to die on the road. Through the actions of the Samaritan who eventually comes to his aid, we see several examples of Biblical generosity.

"But a Samaritan, as he traveled, came where the man was; and when he saw him, he took pity on him. He went to him and bandaged his wounds, pouring on oil and wine. Then he put the man on his own donkey, brought him to an inn and took care of him. The next day he took out two denarii and gave them to the innkeeper. 'Look after him,' he said, 'and when I return, I will reimburse you for any extra expense you may have.'" (Luke 10:33-35)

Obviously, the Samaritan displays *financial* generosity, paying the innkeeper to watch over the injured man and reimbursing him for any extra expenses (v. 35). However, that's not all he does. The parable tells us that the Samaritan "took pity" on the man. He bandages the man, pours oil and wine on him, and takes him to the inn (v. 34). This tremendous personal care demonstrates *relational* generosity. Having already gone above and beyond the call of duty in taking care of a complete stranger, he could have walked away with a clear conscience. Instead, he lets the innkeeper know that he will return to follow-up on the man (v. 35). In this way, he displays generosity with his *time* and *availability*.

It is possible to be financially generous but not relationally generous. For example, I know many who will give financially to churches and organizations that help the homeless but will never stop to engage with a homeless person on the street because it's awkward or pushes them out of their comfort zone.

It is also possible to be relationally generous but not generous with one's time. I have friends who are fantastic people to be around; they're loving, kind, and caring, but it is so difficult to find times when they're available, like being in a friendship with one of those automated phone messages that companies use when they put you on

89

hold, "Your friendship is very important to us, but please wait on the line for a very, very, very, *very* long time."

Through the story of the Good Samaritan, we learn that Scripture calls us to be generous in *all* of these areas.

Moreover, generosity should be practiced with no thought of repayment or reward (Luke 14:12). For example, one year while I was still working as a youth pastor, I decided to rally some friends to make a comedic video to welcome recently graduated high school students to the young adult ministry. Most of the people I asked to star in the video were initially reluctant because they didn't want to look foolish, but after much pushing and persuading, they finally agreed. The video was shown at the first Sunday service that the graduates attended the young adult service, and it was a huge hit. Everyone was raving about it afterwards during fellowship time. The only problem was that hardly anyone knew I had written and directed it (somehow the video editor forgot to add credits). To be frank, I was upset that the people who starred in the video got so much praise afterwards, when in reality, I was the one who invested the most time and energy into the video. I came up with the concept, wrote the script, persuaded everyone to act in it, and was the main driving force behind the project.

As petty as all this sounds, I now faced a tough decision. I could either let people know that I deserved the credit for the video so that I could be exalted by man, *or* I could let it go. I won't let you know what I did because it's not important for this discussion (alright fine, I let it go, but I vented to my wife about it later, *a lot*), but it's an example of how easily a generous and altruistic act can be twisted into something that feeds one's need to be recognized by others. In this way, generosity goes hand in hand with humility. Rick Warren, lead pastor of Saddleback Church in Lake Forest, California and popular Christian author, writes, "Humility is not thinking less of yourself; it is thinking of yourself less."[47] I would personally modify the statement to say, humility is not thinking about yourself *at all*. The truth is, our sinful nature means that the temptation and desire to see ourselves exalted is a struggle we will always face when practicing generosity.

This tension reveals itself in ways both obvious and more subtle. I have a pastor friend who worked at a church in Boston where they would hang up a plaque for every congregation member who gave a significant donation to the ministry. As a result, many would give to the ministry because they wanted to see their names honored on the church walls. Wait, is this too blatantly obvious of an example?

An experience from my days as a youth pastor provides an example of how this temptation can manifest in more subtle ways. An elder of the church once asked me to sit down with him for dinner. He was a very kind man and actually spent most of the meal asking how the adult congregation could assist with our youth ministry, basically a youth pastor's dream come true. After I made a few suggestions, he confidently said to me, "Don't worry about it, David. I'll make sure it gets taken care of."

I was enormously grateful, but I still asked out of curiosity, "How are you going to do that?"

He replied, with a confident smirk, "Don't worry, I've given *a lot* of money to this church over the years."

When Jesus instructs us to be generous without any expectations of a reward (Luke 14:12), this includes even things that we could then use for "good." In the case of this elder, his generous financial giving to the church fostered a sense of self-righteousness that made him feel entitled to dictate how the church operated with regard to the youth ministry. This isn't to say that he doesn't have a right to express his opinions, but the fact remains that his giving did not entitle him to more power or greater authority. His sense of entitlement left no room for humility, and thus it was more likely that he would cause more problems within the church than he solved.

Even when a person's motives appear to be completely selfless, we should carefully examine what's really going on. In J.R.R. Tolkien's *The Lord of the Rings*, the wizard Gandalf refuses to accept the ring of power despite being described as a righteous being.

"No!" cried Gandalf, springing to his feet. "With that power I should have power too great and terrible. And over me the Ring would gain a power still greater and more deadly." His eyes flashed and his face was lit as by a fire within. "Do not tempt me! For I do not wish to become like the Dark Lord himself. Yet the way of the Ring to my heart is by pity, pity for weakness and the desire of strength to do good. Do not

tempt me! I dare not take it, not even to keep it safe, unused."[48]

At first, Gandalf's refusal doesn't seem to make much sense. How could possession of the ring result in him becoming like the Dark Lord Sauron who was the embodiment of evil? After all, by his own admission, Gandalf would use the power of the ring to do good.

Tolkien describes the situation thusly:

"Gandalf as Ring-Lord would have been far worse than (the Dark Lord) Sauron. He would have remained 'righteous', but self-righteous."[49]

Tolkien is saying that although Gandalf was righteous, he too would eventually be corrupted by the ring. The ring would twist Gandalf's righteousness, transforming it to self-righteousness. The danger in self-righteousness is that it makes it harder for us to see our need for a Savior. We become blind to our own sin. If Sauron were to possess the ring of power, his evilness would be obvious to all in the death and destruction that followed in his wake. However, if Gandalf gained that same power, because of his initial desire to use the ring for good, he would not be able to see the ways in which the ring was slowly but surely corrupting him until it was too late, if ever, and thus he would become even more dangerous than Sauron himself.

Now, we've established that generosity should not be practiced with any expectation of repayment or reward. However, that's not all Jesus had to say on the subject.

"But when you give a banquet, invite the poor, the crippled, the lame, the blind, and you will be blessed. Although they cannot repay you, you will be repaid at the resurrection of the righteous." (Luke 14:13-14)

In these verses Jesus clearly states that we *will* receive a reward. The key difference is what the reward is, and who we should look to for our reward. After all, pastors frequently use the word "invest" when asking others to give to Christian causes, and an investment is made with the expectation of some type of return on the investment. However, instead of being generous because we expect an *earthly* return on our investment, our reward will be eternal life through Jesus Christ our Savior. Therefore, being generous as a Christian is not only the right thing to do, but the return on our investment is far greater than anything the world has to offer (Matthew 5:12).

In Victor Hugo's novel *Les Misérables*, Jean Valjean, an ex-convict who is released on parole, is taken in by a kindhearted Bishop who feeds him and gives him a place to stay for the night. However, instead of being grateful, Valjean betrays the Bishop and runs away in the middle of the night having stolen the Bishop's silverware. The next morning, the police catch Valjean and bring him back to the Bishop's home. Having taken advantage of the Bishop's generosity, Valjean is in no position to expect any grace or forgiveness. But instead of revealing Valjean as a thief, the Bishop tells the police that he had given the silverware to Valjean as a gift. Moreover, he doubles down on his kindness and generosity and chides Valjean for leaving behind the candlesticks, which he also claims to have given to Valjean. Stunned by this incredible act of grace, Hugo describes Valjean's reaction as follows:

"Jean Valjean opened his eyes wide, and stared at the venerable Bishop with an expression which no human tongue can render any account of." [50]

Similarly, our relationship with God started out with Him giving us the gift of life. But this was not enough for us, and like Adam and Eve eating from the tree of good and evil (Genesis 3:1-13) and the Israelites in the Old Testament who were repeatedly dissatisfied after God delivered them from slavery in Egypt (Numbers 11:1-15, Exodus 32), we turned away from God and looked to our own idols of pride, materialism, power, and personal ambition. We took advantage of the life He breathed into us by running from Him and seeking our own selfish gains. At this point, we did not deserve any grace, but like the Bishop in *Les Misérables*, God showed us grace anyway. He placed His son Jesus Christ on that cross and treated him in the manner in which we deserved. Christ took on all our sins; he became the one who had run away, he became the one who took advantage of God, he became the betrayer, the creator of idols, the king of lusting after pride, materialism, power, and personal ambition, and he experienced eternal punishment on that cross in our stead so that we could be pardoned for our sins. But God's tremendous act of love didn't end there. He didn't just pardon our sins. He poured in even more kindness and generosity through His son's sacrifice and called us into *royalty* (1 Peter 2:9) so that we don't just escape His wrath if we believe in Jesus, but we also experience the riches of the kingdom of heaven. This was the ultimate act of generosity.

"But God demonstrates his own love for us in this: While we were still sinners, Christ died for us." (Romans 5:8)

Why live a radically generous life with our money, care, and time? The truth is that living generously and giving sacrificially does not come easily to many of us. Our sinful natures desire to be rewarded and acknowledged for our good deeds while still on earth. It is only because of Christ's sacrifice on the cross that we can give without expectation. He has changed the course of our lives and stories forever with *His* generosity, and as such, we should look to change the lives and stories of others with *ours*.

Reflections

If you were to ask me how to build a church, I could share with you everything I know about church systems, administrative work, fundraising, children's ministry, Sunday production, equipment purchases, and advertising. Heck, I even have prior experience in internet search engine optimization. And honestly speaking, all you need is a somewhat compelling leader, an attractive location, and loyal people who are willing to help and you can build a "successful" church if simply enough effort is put in. Yes, sorry to burst your bubble, it's *that* formulaic.

What is not formulaic are the convictions we receive when we live out the gospel. Minus such convictions, church is merely a place we go on Sundays to feel good emotionally or to learn how to be better and more moral people, a place where we meet our friends and hangout, and for families, a place where our kids can play with other kids. Basically, church becomes a social club with a twist.

A few years ago, in North London, a crowd of more than three hundred people began to gather at an "atheist church" called the Sunday Assembly.[51] They sing popular pop songs with a live band (they call it "swapping Psalms for pop songs"), they have a clean cut leader on stage with a button-down shirt and tie who gives inspirational talks and entertains the audience, and of course, they fellowship afterwards together as a community.[52] Functionally, they do pretty much everything a Christian church does, only they aren't

Christians. When we attend church for any other reason than living out the gospel, we have made our churches into the Sunday Assembly.

Which brings me to an incident some years back where an old friend contacted me, asking a series of questions about the church I was attending at the time. He started the conversation by mentioning that he had a newborn and was looking for a church with other newborns so that his child could grow up together with other children. *Check.* Next, he asked how the facility was, if it was large enough to accommodate him and his family. *Check.* Then he asked if there was enough parking. *Check.* Then he asked if the lead pastor was approachable. *Check.* Then he asked if the worship music was too fancy, because he didn't like it when the music was too fancy. *Um, not sure? Check? I think?* Then he asked if the people were friendly, and by this point, I couldn't care less whether he ended up at our church or another church.

I suddenly got sick of playing salesperson. And to be frank, after that incident, I don't care to anymore, *ever.* The truth is, if someone is deciding on a church using a checklist based on external accommodations and criteria, they're probably not interested in a gospel-centered church anyway. The heart of a gospel-centered church is not to put on a show and please man, but to instead live out the gospel by our convictions through prayer and the Word. In fact, the gospel is often offensive to those looking for a comfortable church experience. As Dave Earley, founding pastor of Grace City Church in Las Vegas, Nevada, notes, "The road that Jesus took led him to the cross. If we take the same road, it will lead us to the same place."[53]

Pastors, church leaders, and congregation members must constantly reflect to make sure they are acting out of the gospel, even when we are trying to do "good," or we risk being no different than non-Christian philanthropists. Our acts of love *must* come from Jesus, who freed us from the power of death and opened the way to eternal life.

Edwin Colon, founding pastor of Recovery House of Worship, a network of churches that started in Brooklyn, New York, once spoke about how when he and his family first started planting churches they were so poor they had to sleep at the church. Immediately, they felt convicted by the gospel to invite in the neighborhood homeless. And so for two years while he and his family had no home, they slept in the same place as the homeless. When someone asked why he would do such a thing, his response was simple: "I thought we as Christians were called to do the types of things the early Christians did in the Bible."[54] He said it with a touch of sarcasm, to note the irony of how bizarre, radical, and rare an act like that seems to majority of Christians in the United States today. Meanwhile, it was the norm for those professing their faith in the first century.

This past year, I had lunch with Brian Bakke, the son of Ray Bakke, the Christian author and urban leader who pioneered various movements to help disadvantaged communities. It should be noted that Brian's uncle is Dennis W. Bakke, billionaire entrepreneur and cofounder of AES Corporation. Over our meal, Brian informed me that despite coming from a family of great wealth and popularity, his father raised his kids in the inner city where they ate peanut butter sandwiches every day for lunch. Ray did that so his sons could live with the poor, relate to the poor, and ultimately have compassion for the poor. He speaks of this need to reach the underprivileged in *A Theology as Big as the City*: "More and more wealthy Americans are retreating into 'gated communities' to hold on to the tokens of privilege our society has bestowed on them."[55] He further quotes Raymond Fung, a Christian leader in Hong Kong, regarding his heart for the poor: "The poor are not only sinners; most often they are sinned against."[56]

Many would hear what Ray did with his family and think it was a rather irrational decision. But as Christians, let's think about this carefully. Coming from a position of power to live with the poor, relate to the poor, and have compassion for the poor, that sounds strangely familiar, doesn't it? It is, of course, what Christ did when he came to the earth, which is exactly what the Bible is calling us to be imitators of (Ephesians 5:1-2).

I am not saying we should all rush to become poor. During our Fellows class, when Timothy Keller was asked why he planted a church in the wealthy Upper East Side of Manhattan rather than taking that same funding and planting three churches in poorer neighborhoods, he succinctly replied, "Well, *someone* has to preach the gospel to these people."[57] Which is absolutely true, but it is important to note that he did not plant a church in the Upper East Side because it was nice and comfortable. In fact, during his initial years, his family often had to skip meals because the cost of living was so high relative to his salary. Instead, Keller planted in that region because he had a specific heart, calling, and conviction for the local people. The point is, the gospel convicts in ways that makes us uncomfortable, whether it is inviting inner city teens to our churches, living with the homeless, planting a church in a wealthy area with a relatively modest salary, or as Brian's uncle, Dennis W. Bakke, has pledged, giving up billions of dollars (yes, *billions*, all of his wealth) to church plants through the Mustard Seed Foundation.[58]

So going back to Edwin, after he answered the question of *why* he lived with the homeless, the next question (and perhaps even more baffling one) was *how* he did it. Despite opposition from his friends and family, even after many nights of tears and struggle, he stuck with his convictions. How?

His response to that question was, "I reflected on the Messiah. *A lot.*" He spent time with Jesus, which led him to be an imitator of Jesus. For Edwin, it was the only way he could push through when everyone else was telling him to stop. Because of his years of faithfulness, Recovery House of Worship now has *six* locations across this country, and they minister specifically to people who are/were in recovery and struggling with addiction. Furthermore, the network is one hundred percent funded through outside donations.[59]

But let's tone it down and talk about a man I've encountered who didn't start some impressive movement or give away an enormous amount of money. When my wife suddenly threw out her back one night, my mother called one of her church members named John Woo who came to my house and performed acupuncture on Jany. After he was finished, I gathered some money and asked him how much it would cost for his services. He responded that he could not accept our money. I later discovered that he never accepts money from his patients, that he went to school for eastern medicine while working at his hardware store full time for the sole purpose of doing medical work to help others, free of charge. It was his ministry of generosity. The next time I got injured, he came by again, and as he was performing acupuncture on my knee, I again insisted on paying him. He of course refused, but this time he responded with a cheerful grin, "Don't worry about me David, I'm going to be okay, because what I am doing is nothing compared to what Jesus has done for me."

If the culture of a church is simply aimed at growing numbers but not transforming hearts for Christ, then it is not a gospel-centered church. Similarly, if the culture is directed at feeding people's comfort and not challenging its members, it is not a gospel-centered church. At the core of placing Christ at the center of a ministry is a message that's so powerful it makes us secure enough to be authentic, gracious enough to want to grow alongside a community, driven enough to be missional, curious enough to want to get to know God both intellectually and experientially, accepting enough to be diverse, and radical enough to be generous.

Notes

Introduction

[1] Kristian Hernandez is the Senior Pastor of Hope Astoria. While this quote does not, to our knowledge, appear in a published book, it was spoken by Kristian Hernandez at the New City Gathering on May 18, 2016.

[2] Peter Ahn is the founding and Senior Pastor of Metro Community Church. While this story does not, to our knowledge, appear in a published book, it was spoken by Peter Ahn during the New City Gathering on May 18, 2016.

[3] Dietrich Bonhoeffer, *Life Together: The Classic Exploration of Christian Community* (New York: Harper & Row Publishers, Inc., 1954), p. 37.

[4] Ibid.

[5] *Redeemer City to City*, http://www.redeemercitytocity.com (retrieved October 10, 2016).

Cultural Value #2: Authenticity

[6] Dr. Rob Reimer is the founding and Senior Pastor of Southshore Community Church. While this quote does not, to our knowledge, appear in a published book, it was spoken while he was teaching the Personal, Professional, and Theological Foundations for Ministry course as an adjunct professor in the summer of 2014 at Alliance Theological Seminary, Rockland County Campus.

[7] Dr. Ronald Walborn is the dean of Alliance Theological Seminary. While this quote does not, to our knowledge, appear in a published book, it was spoken while he was teaching the Personal, Professional, and Theological Foundations for Ministry course in the summer of 2014 at the Rockland County Campus.

[8] Bonhoeffer, *Life together,* p. 27.

[9] David Kinnaman & Gabe Lyons, *unChristian: What a New Generation Really Thinks About Christianity...And Why It Matters* (Grand Rapids, MI: BakerBooks,

2007), p. 49-51. Based on research of about 1,000 respondents from ages 16-29 by the California-based research firm The Barna Group.

[10] Jean Vanier, From Brokenness to Community (Mahwah, N.J.: Paulist Press, 1992), p. 16.

[11] Ibid., p. 33.

Cultural Value #3: Community

[12] Justin Bieber, quoted in Joe La Pumba's, *The Deep End: Interview with Justin Bieber, Complex*, http://www.complex.com/music/justin-bieber-interview-2015-cover-story (retrieved August 2, 2016).

[13] Rodney Stark, *The Rise of Christianity: How the Obscure, Marginal Jesus Movement Became the Dominant Religious Force in the Western World in a Few Centuries* (San Francisco: Harper; unknown edition, 1997), pp. 5-6.

[14] Stark, *The Rise of Christianity*, p. 208.

[15] Lisa Wangsness, *An Arlington Evangelical Church Reaches Out*, The Boston Globe, https://www.bostonglobe.com/metro/2012/12/23/highrock-evangelical-church-gives-town-arlington-unusual-christmas-gift-money-pay-social-worker/EjqR TJItlcSHCrVcq1SPzK/story.html (retrieved June 29, 2016).

[16] Ibid.

[17] Ibid.

[18] David Swaim is the Senior Pastor of Highrock. While this quote does not, to the author's knowledge, appear in a published book, it is a frequent saying in his preaching.

[19] Amy Kaufman, Diego Luna, Gael Garcia Bernal (Producers), & Cary Joji Fukunaga (Writer/Director). (2009). *Sin Nombre* [motion picture]. United States-Mexico: Universal Studios Home Entertainment.

[20] Ibid.

Cultural Value #4: Being Missional

[21] Dr. Eric Mason is the founding and Senior Pastor of Epiphany Fellowship. While this quote does not, to the author's knowledge, appear in a published book, it was spoken at City Lab, an event hosted by Redeemer City to City, on January 12, 2017.

[22] Timothy Keller, *Center Church: Doing Balanced, Gospel-Centered Ministry in Your City* (Grand Rapids, MI: Zondervan, 2012), p. 265.

[23] Ibid., p. 274.

[24] Timothy Keller, *The Prodigal God: Recovering the Heart of the Christian Faith* (New York: Penguin Books; Reprint Edition, 2011), pp. 15-6.

[25] While this quote does not, to the author's knowledge, appear in a published book, it was spoken by David Swaim at the New City Gathering on May 17, 2016.

[26] Ibid., p. 96.

27 A.S. Moreau, G.R. Corwin & G.B. McGee, *Introduction to World Missions: A Biblical, Historical, and Practical Survey* (Grand Rapids, MI: Baker Academic, 2004) p. 76.

28 David Gibbons is founding and Senior Pastor of Newsong Church. While this quote does not, to the author's knowledge, appear in a published book, it was spoken when David Gibbons guest spoke at Promise International Fellowship in 2008.

29 William R. Moody, *The Life of Dwight L. Moody, by His Son William R. Moody* (New York: The Authorized Publishers, 1900), p. 503.

Cultural Value #5: Spirit and Truth

30 Douglas Bannister, The Word and Power Church: What Happens When a Church Experiences All God Has to Offer? (Grand Rapids, MI: Zondervan Publishing House, 1999), p. 15.

31 Ibid., p. 20.

32 Jack Deere, Surprised by the Power of the Spirit: Discovering How God Speaks and Heals Today (Grand Rapids, Mich.: Zondervan, 1993), p. 78.

33 Martin Luther, quoted in Roland H. Bainton, Here I Stand: A Life of Martin Luther (Nashville, TN: Abingdon Press; Reprint Edition, 1991), p. 144.

34 Ibid.

35 Kee Won Huh., quoted in *Kee Won Huh's Facebook Page*, https://www.facebook.com/keewonhuh (retrieved August 31, 2016).

36 Paul Ennis, *The Moody Handbook of Theology* (Chicago, IL: Moody Publishers; Revised and Expanded Edition, 1995), p.23.

37 John Piper, quoted in the interview video, *What Cautions Do You Have for the New Reformed Movement?* http://www.desiringgod.org/interviews/what-cautions-do-you-have-for-the-new-reformed-movement (retrieved July 12, 2016).

38 Ibid.

39 Bannister, *The Word and Power Church*, p. 46.

40 Ibid.

Cultural Value #6: Diversity

41 *Youth With a Mission*, http://www.ywam.org (retrieved December 7, 2016).

42 Richard A. Villodas Jr., quoted in *Richard A. Villodas, Jr.'s Facebook Page*, https://www.facebook.com/rvillodas (retrieved July 20, 2016).

43 Bryan Loritts is the Senior Pastor of Abundant Life Christian Fellowship. While this quote does not, to our knowledge, appear in a published book, it was spoken at the New City Gathering on May 18, 2016.

44 Maria W. Kim is a co-editor of *Gospel Culture*. While this quote does not, to our knowledge, appear in a published book, such thoughts were communicated via electronic correspondence with the author.

45 Ibid.

[46] Bruce A. Evans, Raynold Gideon, Andrew Scheinman (Producers), & Rob Reiner (Director). (1986). *Stand by Me* [Motion picture]. United States: Sony Pictures Home Entertainment.

Cultural Value #7: Generosity

[47] Rick Warren, *The Purpose Drive Life* (Grand Rapids, MI: Zondervan, 2002), p. 148.

[48] J.R.R. Tolkien, *The Fellowship of the Ring: Being the First Part of Lord of the Rings* (Boston: Houghton Mifflin Harcourt; 50th Anniversary Edition, 2002), p. 60.

[49] J.R.R. Tolkien quoted in Humphrey Carpenter and Christopher Tolkien, *The Letters of J.R.R. Tolkien, 246 From a Letter to Mrs. Eileen Elgar, Septemeber1963*, Time, https://timedotcom.files.wordpress.com/2014/12/the_letters_of_j.rrtolkien.pdf (retrieved August 26, 2016), 350.

[50] Victor Hugo, *Les Misérables:* (New York: Signet Classic; Unabridged Edition, 1987), p. 105.

Reflections

[51] Brian Wheeler, *What Happens at an Atheist Church? BBC News Magazine,* http://www.bbc.com/news/magazine-21319945 (retrieved August 23, 2016).

[52] *Sunday Assembly*, https://www.sundayassembly.com (retrieved October 31, 2016).

[53] Dave Earley & Rod Dempsey. *Discipleship Making Is...: How to Live the Great Commission with Passion and Confidence* (Nashville: B&H Publishing Group, 2013), p. 87.

[54] Edwin Colon is the founding and Senior Pastor of Recovery House of Worship. While this quote does not, to our knowledge, appear in a published book, it was spoken by Edwin Colon at the New City Gathering on May 17, 2016.

[55] Raymond J. Bakke, *A Theology as Big as the City* (Downers Grove, IL: Intervarsity Press, 1997), p. 59.

[56] Ibid., pp. 42-3 (quoting Raymond Fung, a Baptist Christian leader of Hong Kong).

[57] While this quote does not, to our knowledge, appear in a published book, it was spoken by Dr. Timothy Keller during the Redeemer City to City Fellows Program sometime in the Fall of 2015.

[58] *Mustard Seed Foundation*, http://msfdn.org (retrieved October 16, 2016).

[59] *Recovery House of Worship*, http://www.rhow.org (retrieved September 21, 2016).

Made in the USA
Lexington, KY
09 November 2019